Master Your Real Wealth
How to live your life
with financial security

Erika Penner MFA, CFP, PRP

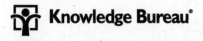

WINNIPEG, MANITOBA, CANADA

Erika Penner

MASTER YOUR REAL WEALTH
How to live your life with financial security

ISBN 978-1-897526-11-8

Printed and bound in Canada

Library and Archives Canada Cataloguing in Publication

Penner, Erika, 1952-
    Master your real wealth: how to live your life
With financial security / Erika Penner.

    1. Finance, Personal—Canada. 2. Financial
security—Canada. 3. Wealth—Canada. 4. Saving
and investment. I. Title.

HG179.R683 2005   332.024'01   C2009-900948-X

Publisher:
Knowledge Bureau, Inc.
Box 52042 Niakwa Postal Outlet, Winnipeg, Manitoba Canada R2M 0Z0
204-953-4769 Email: reception@knowledgebureau.com

Publisher and Managing Editor: Evelyn Jacks
General Manager: Norine Harty
Editorial Assistance: Cordell Jacks and Tamara Baker
Cover and Page Design: Sharon Jones

Acknowledgements

Thank you to my clients who I have the privilege of working with and to my friends and family who have been patient and supportive.

 **Knowledge Bureau®**

Presents
Financial Education for Decision Makers

The Master Your Personal Finances Books:

Master Your Taxes
How to maximize your after-tax returns

Master Your Retirement
How to fulfill your dreams with peace of mind

Master Your Investment in the Family Business
How to increase after-tax wealth

Master Your Money Management
How to manage the advisors who work for you

Master Your Real Wealth
How to live your life with financial security

FREE UPDATING SERVICES

Keep up your Mastery! For the latest in tax and personal financial planning strategies subscribe to Breaking Tax and Investment News. Visit www.knowledgebureau.com/masteryourtaxes

 **Knowledge Bureau®**

Contents

Introduction

This book is intended to help you understand some of key wealth management principles and how to build 'real' wealth—that is, wealth after taxes, costs, inflation and currency risk—so you can prepare to meet the challenges life events can throw at you. The book is also intended to help you decide if working with a financial professional is right for you and if so, to gain an understanding of some important issues in the financial world so that you feel more comfortable asking the right questions about accumulating, growing, preserving and eventually transitioning your real wealth.

This is important. Money strikes a cord in all of us—good or bad. As a financial professional, working with money is second nature to me. But when I have to deal with health-related matters, for example, I feel like I've entered a brand new world. The language is different and new, and so are the processes and procedures. It's difficult to make decisions when you are a neophyte; fortunately my health care professionals work with me to make the right decisions for my health. I realized when I was speaking with my health care professionals, that's how they feel about the financial world!

Understanding the financial world means all the advisors on your financial team must have a common language, which they share with you. And they must have a common tool to measure outcomes.

That's why, in this book, we will review the important information present in your Personal Net Worth Statement with you. It's the cornerstone to building your wealth, and a statement all of your professionals will understand, whether that's your banker, investment advisor, tax advisor or lawyer. Most important, the Personal Net Worth Statement will help you quickly identify areas where changes are needed and can help track progress of your wealth creation and preservation activities over time.

You will also learn what issues to consider when reviewing recommendations your investment advisors have for financial products, and how to manage the risk you are comfortable in taking in building your net worth. We'll arm you with pertinent and detailed information on the major threats to your 'real' wealth—things like taxes and inflation and the costs you pay to your money managers.

You should know that financial planning is a large field that is constantly changing. Staying current with economic and tax changes, new products and methods of investing is a full-time job. But the principles of financial security don't change that much. Understand the basics of Real Wealth Management™ and you can work with the best options available to you and your family!

THE FORMAT OF THIS BOOK

The principles for Mastering Your Real Wealth are discussed in this book in a straight-forward fashion, with common features to empower you. In each chapter you will find:

- *A True to Life Scenario:* These feature fictitious families in real-life situations and are a backdrop for the principles discussed in the chapter.
- *The Issues:* What is important and why?

- *The Solutions:* What do you need to know and do to make the right financial decisions for your time and money? How can you best integrate these solutions in your strategic plan to meet goals by asking the right questions?
- *The Mastery:* Tips and Traps to help you put your financial decision making into focus, simplify your efforts, and get better results.

I trust you'll find this format useful in taking control and making better financial decisions either on your own, or together with your team of financial advisors.

ERIKA PENNER AND
THE KNOWLEDGE BUREAU

CHAPTER 1

Why is This Book Important to You?

You can be young without money, but you can't be old without it.
TENNESSEE WILLIAMS

I've known Candace and Roger for 10 years, as their friend and more recently as their financial planner. Their passion for living in the moment is contagious. With Roger a history buff and Candace a "clotheshorse", frequent trips to Europe satisfy both of their interests.

Roger has been employed in the health field for over 20 years, enjoying an income of over $130,000 annually. Candace is self-employed as a graphic designer and takes home about $60,000 per year. They decided long ago not to have children and are now both in their mid-40's.

Last month Candace asked me to meet with her... it seems they are over limit on their credit cards; they have been making no headway on their mortgage and have recently been declined by their bank for a loan to buy a vacation property.

THE ISSUES

How can it be possible that a couple earning close to $200,000 together have no savings and are in fact, not credit worthy?

As a financial planner, I have encountered these types of situations before and was not surprised by their financial crisis. While the couple enjoys a better than average combined income compared to most people, they have not been saving anything. They are of the opinion that building up the equity in their home will give them the financial security they will need later in life. The problem is, with no savings and all current income being "enjoyed", they are not protecting their current financial position nor are they building one for the future. This couple has all their eggs in one financial basket, and a blind eye to diversifying away risk.

It gets worse. The trips they pay for with their credit cards and the clothes that Candace likes buying do nothing to build their financial equity. These are things—things that are "used up"—depreciating in value the moment they leave the store to be enjoyed today. While they may perhaps provide happy memories at some point, they will not help to build home equity or put food on the table. Should Candace lose her job before paying off her credit cards, her very expensive non-deductible interest charges will become a significant burden.

Today's baby boomers, aided by parents who wanted them to have a better life than they had and supported by government social programs, often take for granted their ability to use their incomes for lifestyle choices, rather than putting money aside for a rainy day. Moreover, many are not aware of how to maximize their financial position by taking advantage of some very simple financial planning strategies. These changed values, and lack of financial literacy, have been passed down to their children as well.

These are big issues. The facts are that many in today's generation are expected to live as long in retirement as the years they spent working. Therefore, paying attention to wealth creation and management can make a world of difference throughout a family's lifecycle. In the absence of wealth management, people's choices narrow and standards of living can change suddenly and not always in the right direction.

THE SOLUTIONS

There are five basic solutions everyone needs to know and understand in order to create sustainable real wealth over time.

- The difference between income and real wealth accumulation.
- How to manage life events with your finances.
- The importance of financial self-reliance in the future.
- The concept of longevity risk.
- How to work well with your professional financial advisor.

UNDERSTAND THE DIFFERENCE BETWEEN INCOME AND REAL WEALTH ACCUMULATION

Income is the cash flow you realize by working, receiving investment income, renting out a property or perhaps enjoying a pension after many years of working. People have lots of choices on how to use that income. Income that is used to purchase a "lifestyle" does not necessarily contribute to your real wealth.

A car that is leased, for example, uses some of your cash flow each month but that does not contribute to the value of your asset base—there is no ownership of the asset. Even if you purchase your vehicle, you must accept that it is a depreciating asset and does not help to build your net worth. Not only that, your choice may bring you pleasure, but only in the short term. Studies show the pleasure of owning a new car wears off in three to six months—so be sure there are other valid reasons for choosing a new vehicle instead of a slightly used one. Once the money is spent, it cannot be saved. That limits your options for creating wealth for future choices.

It's not surprising to me that individuals with a lower income often do a better job of saving. After all, they have most likely learned to live within a budget and know the difference between what they need to have versus what they would *like to have*.

The benefits of saving a dollar rather than spending it are twofold. First, a dollar *spent* is actually worth $1.30 or more, after tax and depending on the province in which you live. Secondly, a dollar saved can be put to work compounding and growing for you immediately, often on a lucrative before-tax basis.

For example, in British Columbia the top marginal tax rate for salaried income at the time of writing was 43.7%. So if I decide I want to spend $1,000 on a new bicycle, with money I have earned and paid taxes on, the $1,000 bicycle actually costs me $1,437.00.

If, instead, I decide to take the public transit a bit longer, and put that $1,000 into an RRSP (Registered Retirement Savings Plan) which earns interest @ 5% on a compounding basis over five years, that $1,000 will have grown to $1,276.28 (and that's not taking into account the tax deduction I am eligible for because of the RRSP contribution ($437.00, each year) and the deductible cost of the public transit passes!) If I invest wisely, my tax savings from the RRSP alone can help me buy a fancy used bike using what is essentially new money.

You can see that the choices I make on how I spend my money can be more expensive, or more productive, depending on how I use my after-tax dollars.

Real wealth starts with the after tax money you have, net of all debt. Do you know what your real wealth is today?

UNDERSTANDING HOW TO MANAGE LIFE EVENTS WITH YOUR FINANCES

Use Your Money to Manage Your Life

Your money is there to help you manage life events. Recognizing and preparing for such situations can help you make more appropriate choices with your cash flow.

Money not allocated easily disappears into thin air. Some people find that if they carry cash in their wallets, they are more cautious about how they spend it; others find they spend actual cash much faster than if they use some other form of payment. You need to know what works for you.

Many people also fall into the trap of using too much credit. If you use credit cards to make purchases and don't pay them off in full each month, you are incurring a very large, non-deductible interest expense. Since these debts are paid off with after-tax dollars, a credit card rate of 18% translates into 22.5% or more, depending on your tax bracket. It is often the many little things and the unplanned big-ticket items that can place your finances in a precarious position. Remember there are two precious factors in play in building real wealth: time and money.

Manage Your Savings

An understanding of how much time it takes for you to make money—before taxes—to fund your expenditures is important. We often work harder than we think for items of little or no value, as we discussed earlier. Therefore it's important to know how to save, and for what.

A young family will have more difficulty setting up a savings program as the cost of raising children continues to grow, particularly when you consider the heightened importance of young adults completing a university education or becoming skilled in a trade. Fortunately there are numerous tax-preferred investment vehicles available to help fund a child's education. The family must simply understand what savings plans to fund first when after-tax dollars are available.

What is also important is to *continue to save*. That is, when you achieve your goals with enough money saved for your children's education, you should start to put that same monthly "savings room" in your budget towards something else like your retirement savings, or against your mortgage. (Perhaps you want to do a combination of all three at the same time. You may need to ask your financial advisors to help you with this.)

Manage Your Personal Risks

In building real wealth, you also need to think about managing risk. Insurance, in all of its permutations, is the most disliked word I seem to come across. Why is insurance an important component of wealth management? When you consider that your largest lifetime asset is your income and that income is what will build your net worth, why would you not ensure your net worth is protected?

We purchase insurance to protect our investment in our cars but often we don't worry about fire insurance or life insurance. Insurance may well be one of your most liquid assets when you are young and a catastrophe happens. As we get older, insurance can be used to protect the value of our assets (e.g. critical illness insurance), to see us through a much longer retirement period (e.g. long term care insurance) or to pass an inheritance along to our loved ones or favourite charity (e.g. life insurance). Investing in insurance provides an opportunity to use someone else's money to protect and extend your personal productivity.

Let's look at the following example. If you currently earn $50,000 per year and you can expect an annual increase of 2%, your income over the next 25 years will total a little over $1.6 million. In most cases, this is significantly larger than any car or house purchase you will make.

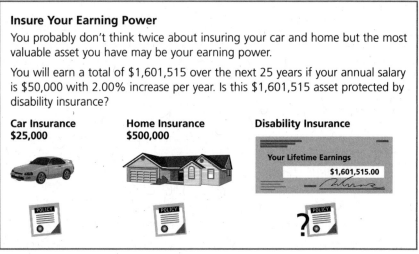

Insure Your Earning Power

You probably don't think twice about insuring your car and home but the most valuable asset you have may be your earning power.

You will earn a total of $1,601,515 over the next 25 years if your annual salary is $50,000 with 2.00% increase per year. Is this $1,601,515 asset protected by disability insurance?

Car Insurance
$25,000

Home Insurance
$500,000

Disability Insurance

Your Lifetime Earnings
$1,601,515.00

POLICY

POLICY

? POLICY

Source: Ativa Concept Toolkit 9 (www.ativa.com)

In addition, accidents and illnesses are a fact of life. They could happen to anyone at any time. Did you know that one in three people, on average, will be disabled for 90 days or longer at least once before age 65? And if you are unfortunate enough to be disabled for over 90 days, the average length of such a disability is 2.9 years.

So if you have now been working for 10 years and have been earning $50,000/year indexed annually @ 2%, your income today is $60,950.

If you become disabled and are off work for 2.9 years, you will lose a little over $186,000 during that time period. Can you see how it's much easier to recover from damage to an uninsured vehicle (and sometimes a house) than from an uninsured loss of income?

Manage Your Taxes

As you start to earn a better income, managing your tax bill is one of the best ways to maximize your income and net worth. Choosing tax efficient investment products, taking advantage of tax credits, reducing the amount of tax you pay—all of these strategies take a bit more time and effort to plan but do not cost any more money. *You are entitled to arrange your affairs to pay the least amount of tax that is required.*

Canada's tax system is progressive—that is, the more you earn the more income taxes you pay—in theory. In British Columbia, if you earn $75,000 for 25 years, increased by 2% each year, your gross lifetime earning over that period will be $2,402,272. At an average tax rate of 22.77%, you will pay income taxes of $546,990 over the same period. In fact, many of us work almost ¹/₂ year simply to pay our income taxes. Personal income taxes can be one of your greatest life expenses. It makes sense to find legal ways to minimize this cost.

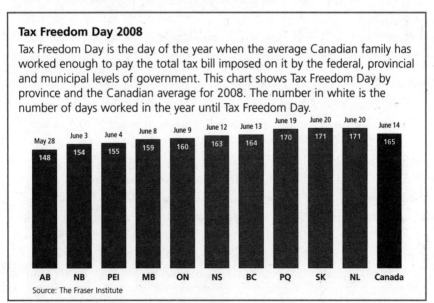

Tax Freedom Day 2008

Tax Freedom Day is the day of the year when the average Canadian family has worked enough to pay the total tax bill imposed on it by the federal, provincial and municipal levels of government. This chart shows Tax Freedom Day by province and the Canadian average for 2008. The number in white is the number of days worked in the year until Tax Freedom Day.

AB	NB	PEI	MB	ON	NS	BC	PQ	SK	NL	Canada
May 28	June 3	June 4	June 8	June 9	June 12	June 13	June 19	June 20	June 20	June 14
148	154	155	159	160	163	164	170	171	171	165

Source: The Fraser Institute

Source: Ativa Concept Toolkit 9 (www.ativa.com)

Manage Your Relationships

One of the most financially devastating life events can be a divorce later in life and that is a phenomenon that is on the increase. In the U.S., the leading edge of baby boomers—those born between 1946 and 1955—has the highest divorce rate amongst Americans. Similar patterns are being noticed by financial planners in Canada. With a late in life divorce, not only have your retirement dreams been turned on their head, there is less time to rebuild your net worth. Ensuring the division of assets and income is correctly structured for each partner as they begin their new lives is critical, yet often there is little real thought given to how such a division will play out in the future. And such agreements can often not be undone or only by incurring more costs.

THE IMPORTANCE OF FINANCIAL SELF-RELIANCE IN THE FUTURE

Planning for security in retirement is a lifelong endeavour for many people. There are several ways to get there, depending on your circumstances.

Today, fewer workers can expect a defined pension plan when they retire. Instead, more and more people are expected to save for their future through a combination of defined contribution plans and tax preferred savings plans like the Registered Retirement Savings Plans (RRSPs). The market risk, in these cases, is assumed by the individual.

While there are some social programs that can help (such as Canada Pension Plan, Old Age Security and Guaranteed Income Supplement for lower-income Canadians) and these programs seem to be financially secure at the time of writing, they have been established to replace approximately 25% of the income you enjoy while working. Some recent studies have indicated that Canadians are on track to replace only 50% of their pre-retirement income (including CPP and OAS)[1]. That, coupled with an uncertainty as to how much income will really be needed in retirement, ensures that each Canadian is increasingly being required to take personal responsibility for their own, often very long, retirement. The time to get serious about saving more money for your future is now.

---

[1]Source: The 2007 Fidelity Retirement Index (Reproduced with permission from Fidelity Investments Canada ULC)

UNDERSTANDING THE CONCEPT OF LONGEVITY RISK

Not only are individuals living longer as a result of medical advances, our population is also aging overall, impacting the country's demographics and services available to our society.

Because of extended lifelines, many of today's boomers fall into the "sandwich generation"—those individuals caring for their children and aging parents. Their parents, if frail of health, may need increasing care— which can mean additional costs or time commitments. For boomers' children, there are fewer full-time jobs available as well as an increased need for education. As a result, for many boomers the idea of saving for an extended retirement and maintaining their lifestyle may seem an impossible task—unless that is taken into consideration during the planning process.

A longer life means not only that you need to save money for a longer period of time but also, that in some of those years your health may be impacted, resulting in substantial health care or residential care costs. In 2004-05, one out of 30 seniors aged 65 years and older lived in one of Canada's 1,952 homes for the aged[2]. Various studies have shown that *between ¹/₃ and ¹/₂ of a person's lifetime healthcare expenditures occur during the final year of life.*[3]

LEARNING HOW TO WORK WELL WITH YOUR PROFESSIONAL FINANCIAL ADVISOR

A recurring theme in our introduction of Real Wealth Management™ is the need for every individual to plan for and mitigate risk with proper planning. This means, for example, making certain you are not over-insured but correctly insured. Or it may entail looking at your invest-ment asset allocation and comparing it to your risk profile. To help you with risk management, which will ultimately help you to accumulate, grow, use and transition your wealth, there may be the need for specific expertise which you may not have.

[2]Source: Statistics Canada, The Daily, May 30, 2007 (http://www.statcan.gc.ca/daily-quotidien/070530/dq070530d-eng.htm)
[3]Source: Canadian Centre for Policy Alternatives, Editorial, November 7, 2006

You could be the type of individual that enjoys doing your own research and your own investing. Or perhaps you worked with a financial advisor previously and found it to be an unsatisfactory situation. Even do-it-yourselfers, though, find the need to access another person's expertise from time to time—knowing how to choose that person and working with him or her can be crucial to your sense of having made the most of the relationship and accomplished what you set out to do.

A good place to start choosing a financial professional is to ask family and friends for the name of the person they work with. They may be able to tell you why they chose that person and what some of their previous experiences have been. While this is a good starting point, that person may not necessarily be the right professional for you. Your needs may be different or you may work better with someone who has a different type of personality. But you may have learned some questions to ask. Several of the Canadian mutual fund companies have a list of issues to consider and ask when choosing your financial professional. These are available on their public web sites and offer some good suggestions.

I am a strong believer in credentials—that is, has the person done the hard work in order to call themselves a financial professional. If you are looking for someone to help you in a comprehensive manner with your finances, choosing someone who has earned the Certified Financial Planner (CFP) designation is important. You can find a list of CFPs in good standing on the Financial Planners Standards Council (FPSC) website (www.fpsccanada.org). This is the body that licenses the CFP and establishes and enforces the standards of competency, practice and ethics for the CFP. This site, too, offers some good suggestions on what to look for when selecting someone to work with you.

You may also wish to seek someone who has an MFA (Master Financial Advisor) or DFA (Distinguished Financial Advisor) designation. This person has been trained to work on an inter-advisory team as a specialist in either retirement income planning, investment income planning, tax and estate planning, or bookkeeping for owner-managers. For more information, visit www.knowledgebureau.com. The FPSC and several other professional and accrediting bodies recognize the courses within the MFA and DFA programs for continuing education purposes.

Along with credentials comes experience. Someone newer in the business but who works in the financial planning arena may well offer you more expertise than someone who has a list of letters behind his or her name but has never completed a financial plan. You also want to work with someone who understands your demographics. In other words, if the financial professional primarily works with individuals who earn a salary but you are self-employed, find out what sort of knowledge he or she has that relates to your situation. If the financial professional is engaged in 'lifetime' learning, he or she will usually have the resources required to be able to offer you the expertise you need.

Remember that not all financial advisors are the same, much as there are differences between physicians, dentists, lawyers, contractors, plumbers or other people you might hire to help you out. Once you have established their expertise, choosing the right person is much like looking for someone you are prepared to enter into a relationship with. Trust is paramount but so are integrity, compatibility, reliability, the ability to communicate and a sense of being comfortable asking the questions you need answers to. Your financial professional is there to work with you and help you understand how your decisions may impact your financial goals. It is a partnership in which each party has his or her own set of responsibilities.

To Master Your Real Wealth, it's important that both you and your most trusted advisors know you and your vision and values well.

IN SUMMARY

THINGS YOU NEED TO KNOW

- Protecting your current financial position, by saving money, is important.
- When you put no thought into building wealth for the future, your lifestyle is exposed to risk.
- Putting all your eggs into one financial basket can limit your choices.
- Investing in "depreciating" consumer goods will erode your wealth.
- Paying expensive credit card interest for depreciating goods erodes your future income.
- Retirement may be a long period: paying attention to wealth creation and management can help you make the choices you want when you can't work any more.

QUESTIONS YOU NEED TO ASK

- What is the difference between income and real wealth accumulation?
- What is the tax cost of every dollar I spend?
- What is the tax cost of every dollar I save?
- What are the tax-preferred investments I should consider investing in?
- What is my real wealth today?
- Should I buy insurance to manage personal risk?
- How much income will I need in retirement?
- Should I seek professional advice to manage my real wealth?

THINGS YOU NEED TO DO

- Create a budget based on your after-tax income.
- Save more money.
- Pay less credit card interest.
- Invest in more appreciating assets, less depreciating assets.
- Manage the credit you use.
- Understand how time and money can help you create real wealth.

DECISIONS YOU NEED TO MAKE

- Decide on a specific amount of money you want to save every month.
- Decide how much you will need to retire with, taking into account personal risks like relationship or health breakdowns and lifestyle wants and needs.
- Decide to pay less tax.
- Decide to get out of debt.
- Decide to convert non-deductible interest payments into savings.
- Look into the appropriateness of insurance for yourself and your family.

Principle Mastery: Real Wealth Management™ focuses on what's left after tax, inflation and costs. Simply put, it is a process that helps you get the real money you need for your lifestyle now and in the future. To get more of it, you need to understand the value of every dollar spent and saved, and how to do so tax efficiently. Getting help with that and your investing and debt management activities from a professional advisory team will help you protect your personal productivity, and that of your money over time.

MASTER YOUR REAL WEALTH
Why is This Book Important to You?

TIPS

- Use your income to acquire assets that will help build, not erode, your real wealth: after tax, after costs, after inflation and after currency risk.
- Recognize that each life event has some financial component and prepare for it.
- Understand that every expenditure has a tax cost.
- Use other people's money (insurance) to protect your assets and income.
- Preparing for the future is increasingly your responsibility.
- Select your financial professional as you would any other professional—their credentials, experience, attitude and compatibility.

TRAPS

- Don't put all your eggs in one basket: understand the risks you face and diversify them away or at least mitigate them.
- Don't spend recklessly—circumstances change. Always be prepared for a rainy day.
- Our retirement can be as long or longer than our working lives, therefore, don't just guess at what your financial needs will be. Do some planning.
- Don't look at lifestyle as a gauge of financial health.
- Don't consider lines of credit as cash flow—these are often the quickest way to get into financial trouble.
- There is "good" and "bad" debt—know the difference.
- Not doing any tax planning can mean that Canada Revenue Agency is better off from your working than you are.
- Don't go it alone. A financial team comprised of a financial planner, insurance specialist, accountant and lawyer may be required in various life stages and can bring value that will really pay off.

CHAPTER 2

What is "Real" Wealth?

I don't think you can spend yourself rich. GEORGE HUMPHREY

Marjorie is a salaried professional, 40 years old, and earning $150,000 per year. She is not allowed to incorporate, which might have enabled her to reduce and defer taxes if she does not need all her income to live on. Consequently, she is being taxed personally at the highest marginal tax rate.

She is a good saver, having 'maxed out' her Registered Retirement Savings Plan (RRSP) contributions each year. She is also saving an additional $1,000 each month in a non-registered investment account.

At the start of the year her investment advisor suggested several changes to her portfolio and while she agreed with the reasons for making the changes, she now realizes that the tax impact of the changes was not considered. The end result is that she now has a taxable capital gain to report in her income and because she doesn't have any capital losses from previous years to offset against this amount, she will have to pay a large sum in additional income taxes when she files her tax return. The actual capital she is left with is much less than she and her advisor anticipated, something she feels her advisor should have talked to her about, given her specific goals for the money.

THE ISSUES

The issues for individuals such as Marjorie are significant. Marjorie—and her advisor—need to understand the impact taxes and other factors can have on the accumulation of real wealth so that the actual dollars she is left with can fund her wants and needs.

I have worked with many clients whose former financial advisor suggested making changes to their portfolios without considering the impact of income taxes on those recommendations. As a result, I have seen seniors have their Old Age Security (OAS) "clawed back"; another disabled individual was cut off government social assistance payments; still another needed to borrow money in order to pay the income taxes due. These are unanticipated results that not only erode wealth and put pressure on a diminished portfolio to generate even more income, often with more risk, than the client anticipated taking later in life.

In Marjorie's case, for example, an annual pension of $80,000 will be receivable if she retires at age 60. At that time she plans to move all of her investments into Guaranteed Investment Certificates (GICs) so that she doesn't have to worry about market fluctuations. She and her advisor calculated that her investments, converted to GICs at that time, will generate another $20,000 in income, which will allow her to receive income of $100,000, an amount she feels will be sufficient to live the type of retirement she has in mind.

However, Marjorie's advisor has not calculated the tax impact—all of her income will be taxed at the same high marginal tax rate. Neither was the effect inflation will have on her purchasing power taken into account. Since her pension is not indexed (that is, it doesn't increase with inflation), at age 60 she may well have sufficient income. But if her expenses increase by 2% each year, by age 65 she will have a $10,000 shortfall—unless her GICs pay out that much more when she retires—an unlikely scenario.

Therefore, it is important for Marjorie and her advisors to understand what real wealth is, why it is important to accumulate it with strategy and process and what factors can negatively impact its growth and transition to the next generation, as life circumstances, capital markets and taxes changes over time.

THE SOLUTIONS

There are 4 primary factors to consider when managing your real wealth.

- The impact of taxes.
- The negative impact of inflation.
- Currency risk.
- Intergenerational transfer of wealth.

UNDERSTAND THE IMPACT OF TAXES

Regardless of the tax bracket you are in, it is important to know that taxes can affect you in two significant ways:

Different types of income are taxed at different rates—and that means the amount of income you keep will be different, depending on the nature of that income. The *Marginal Tax Rate* (MTR) is a term you will often hear associated with how income is taxed: this is the amount of tax you will pay on the next dollar of income. Look at the results of how $90,000 earned in different parts of Canada will be taxed, depending on the type of income that is received:

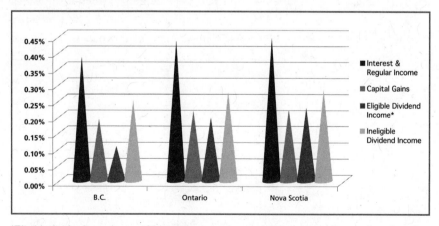

*Eligible dividends are those paid by public corporations and private companies out of earnings that have been taxed at the general corporate tax rate. Your tax slip will indicate if your dividends are "eligible" or "ineligible".

It becomes quite clear that if you can find a way to change or *diversify* the type of income you earn, you will be able to keep more of that income in your pocket.

For example, if you are an employee, you will normally earn a salary which will be taxed as "regular" income, fully taxable. There is often little you can do to change that, although the Income Tax Act provides you with the opportunity to write off certain expenses of employment in some cases, or negotiate for tax free and taxable perks which use your employer's capital to enable a better lifestyle. You however, might be able to change the type of income you earn from your investments to average down the taxes you pay when your tax-paid dollars are reinvested.

For instance, assuming you have a non-registered investment account, consider the various tax results of the income you earn. If you have money invested in Money Market (MM) funds and one type of fund generates interest income while the other pays capital gains, the amount of money you get to keep after taxes will be significantly different, depending on your Marginal Tax Rate. Take the case of an employee earning a $90,000 salary and who has invested in two MM funds, one of which earns $20,000 in interest income and one which earns $20,000 in capital gains. The after-tax income the employee gets to keep is about $4,000 higher when received by way of capital gains instead of interest income. That's because only $^1/_2$ of the capital gain is taxable.

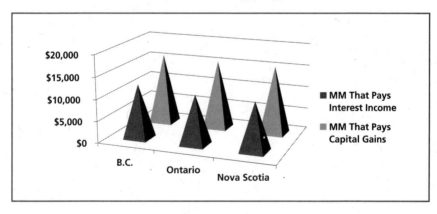

This is an example of *tax efficiency planning—a strategy used to keep investment capital away from the taxman*. A tax efficient focus allows you to take a close look at the impact of taxes on the investments in a taxable investment portfolio.

For greater clarity, know that investors can deposit funds into a "registered" or "non-registered account" with different results.

Consider first the tax results on your investment income, when you invest funds in a "registered account" like an Registered Retirement Savings Plan (RRSP), Registered Education Savings Plan (RESP) or Tax-Free Savings Plan (TFSP). These types of plans allow income to be earned tax free within the plan—there is no tax payable until the money is withdrawn. In the case of the TFSP, there is no tax payable even at withdrawal provided the terms of the program have been adhered to. In the case of the RRSP you are also allowed to invest on a pre-tax basis, which means that you received a tax deduction for the principal at the time of investment provided that you have qualifying earned income and are age eligible.

The level of trading activity in the investment portfolio can also have a tax consequence. For instance, consider an investment that does not pay any income versus an investment that pays out a monthly dividend or capital gain; the former will have a much reduced (if not zero) tax scenario for you. Combining investment performance with income "realization" options, brings you a better average after-tax results, which means, you get to keep more of the investment earnings your portfolio makes.

Similarly, if you purchase a mutual fund in a non-registered portfolio and it has a high turnover of holdings, even if you keep the fund for the long term, each year you may receive a tax slip for capital gains/losses that are created when the various holdings are replaced. This can not only affect your cash flow from the investment, but also whether or not you'll need to make quarterly tax instalments to the government, which will require you to tap into capital growing in the portfolio. It is important to understand this when you consider where to invest your money, and something your advisors should discuss with you.

It is therefore important that your financial advisor has a close working relationship with your tax advisor, to get the results you need, with a "no surprises" approach.

UNDERSTAND THE
NEGATIVE IMPACT OF INFLATION

All of us have experienced the impact of increased gas and food prices on our budgets—or if you don't have a budget, on how much money you have left at the end of the month. Entire industries are being transformed as consumers move away from owning SUVs and are being more selective in the foods they buy. The average retail cost in Vancouver, for example, for 2 litres of ice cream increased from $4.90 in 2004 to $5.49 in 2008[1]—a 10.29 % increase. Many premium brands have increased by more than that!

Inflation is a persistent rise over time in the average price of goods and services—the "cost of living". The most widely used measure is the Consumer Price index which provides a wide measure of the cost of living in Canada. Since December 1993 the Government of Canada and Bank of Canada have agreed to a target inflation range of 1-3%, with the mid-point of 2% being the goal. Over the past 40 years, Canada's average inflation rate has varied. It reached a high of 12.4% in 1981 but has been more or less in the target range since 1992.

Why is this important? Even when inflation is relatively low, as it has been over the past decade and a half, it can erode savings if your investments do not generate returns that can outpace the cost of living. And, the effect on your real wealth is astounding.

For instance, if inflation is currently at 2% per year and your $100,000 GIC earns you 4.5% each year for 5 years, your net return on that investment at the end of that 5 year period is $22,297.45 (2.5%) versus the $24,618.19 you would have earned if inflation had not been a factor.

---

[1]Source: Statistics Canada with calculations done by AAFC-AID, Dairy Section (http://www.dairyinfo.gc.ca/pdf/retail_prices_icecream_e.pdf)

Another way to understand the impact of inflation, from today's stand-point, is to look at your income needs. If you know you will need $90,000 income in 10 years time, with 2% inflation, that $90,000 is equivalent to a salary of $73,381.35 today[2]. Would you be able to manage on that income today? How will you manage in the future without taking inflation into account in your savings strategies?

UNDERSTAND CURRENCY RISK

Many investors understand the need for investing in different geographic areas. Doing so opens up the 97% of the world's markets and helps you gain exposure to many of the world's best companies. And, after all, no one market performs the best each and every year—just look at the chart on page 32.

Most foreign investments are, however, purchased in currencies other than the Canadian dollar. As a result, the value of those investments will be affected by changes in the value of the Canadian dollar relative to foreign currencies.

In 2002, the Canadian dollar versus the U.S. dollar hit an all time low (Jan. 21, 2002) of $1 CAN = $0.6179 U.S.[3] The highest point was reached on July 7, 2007 of $1 CAN = $1.1030 U.S.[3]

While it was a good time to travel in the US with high value Canadian dollars, unfortunately, the impact on investments was not as good: as the Canadian dollar increased in value against the U.S. dollar the value of the U.S. dollar investments actually declined for Canadians. As a result, even when the U.S. markets were performing well, many Canadian investors experienced a negative return on their U.S. investments. Currency risk, therefore, must be taken into account when determining your real wealth.

In some cases, currencies may be hedged, which is a means of reducing the impact that a change in exchange rates may have on the value of the

[2]Source: Bank of Canada Investment Calculator (http://www.bankofcanada.ca/en/rates/investment.html)
[3]Source: Bank of Canada Exchange Rates (http://www.bankofcanada.ca/en/rates/can_us_lookup.html)

The Best Performing Asset Classes Change from Year to Year

1992	1993	1994	1995	1996	1997	1998	1999	2000	2001	2002	2003	2004	2005	2006	2007
US Small Cap 30.5%	Emerging Markets 82.3%	Int'l Equities 14.5%	US Large Cap 33.9%	Cdn Small Cap 28.7%	US Large Cap 39.2%	US Large Cap 37.7%	Emerging Markets 57.2%	Cdn Bonds 10.3%	US Small Cap 8.8%	Cdn Bonds 8.7%	Cdn Small Cap 42.7%	Emerging Markets 16.8%	Emerging Markets 31.2%	Emerging Markets 31.2%	Emerging Markets 38.7%
Emerging Markets 22.4%	Cdn Small Cap 48.3%	Global Equities 11.9%	US Small Cap 24.9%	Cdn Large Cap 28.4%	US Small Cap 27.7%	Global Equities 33.7%	Cdn Large Cap 31.7%	Cdn Large Cap 7.4%	Cdn Bonds 8.1%	Cdn Small Cap -0.9%	Emerging Markets 27.8%	Cdn Large Cap 14.5%	Cdn Large Cap 24.1%	Int'l Equities 26.8%	Cdn Large Cap 9.8%
US Large Cap 18.4%	Int'l Equities 38.5%	US Large Cap 7.4%	Cdn Bonds 20.7%	US Large Cap 23.4%	Global Equities 21.3%	Int'l Equities 28.9%	Cdn Small Cap 20.3%	Cdn Small Cap 7.3%	Emerging Markets 3.8%	Emerging Markets -7.0%	Cdn Large Cap 26.7%	Cdn Small Cap 14.1%	Cdn Small Cap 19.7%	Global Equities 20.6%	Cdn Bonds 3.7%
Cdn Bonds 9.8%	Cdn Large Cap 32.6%	US Small Cap 4.0%	Global Equities 18.1%	US Small Cap 16.9%	Cdn Large Cap 15.0%	Cdn Bonds 9.2%	Int'l Equities 20.1%	US Small Cap 0.8%	Cdn Small Cap 3.4%	Cdn Large Cap -12.4%	US Small Cap 20.5%	Int'l Equities 12.4%	Int'l Equities 10.5%	US Small Cap 18.3%	Cdn Small Cap 2.0%
Cdn Small Cap 9.7%	Global Equities 28.3%	Cdn Large Cap -0.2%	Cdn Large Cap 14.5%	Global Equities 14.4%	Cdn Bonds 9.6%	US Small Cap 4.4%	Global Equities 19.2%	US Large Cap -5.5%	US Large Cap -6.5%	Int'l Equities -16.4%	Int'l Equities 13.9%	US Small Cap 10.2%	Global Equities 6.6%	Cdn Large Cap 17.3%	Int'l Equities -5.3%
Global Equities 4.9%	US Small Cap 23.9%	Emerging Markets -1.8%	Cdn Small Cap 13.9%	Cdn Bonds 12.3%	Cdn Small Cap 7.0%	Cdn Large Cap -1.6%	US Small Cap 14.4%	Global Equities -9.5%	Global Equities -11.4%	Global Equities -20.2%	Global Equities 9.4%	Global Equities 7.3%	Cdn Bonds 6.5%	Cdn Small Cap 16.6%	Global Equities -7.1%
Cdn Large Cap -1.4%	Cdn Bonds 18.1%	Cdn Bonds -4.3%	Int'l Equities 8.6%	Int'l Equities 6.7%	Int'l Equities 6.5%	Cdn Small Cap -17.9%	US Large Cap 14.2%	Int'l Equities -10.6%	Cdn Large Cap -12.6%	US Small Cap -21.1%	Cdn Bonds 6.7%	Cdn Bonds 7.2%	US Large Cap 1.6%	US Large Cap 15.7%	US Large Cap -10.6%
Int'l Equities -3.0%	US Large Cap 14.7%	Cdn Small Cap -8.6%	Emerging Markets -7.8%	Emerging Markets 6.6%	Emerging Markets -7.7%	Emerging Markets -19.9%	Cdn Bonds -1.1%	Emerging Markets -28.2%	Int'l Equities -16.4%	US Large Cap -22.7%	US Large Cap 5.3%	US Large Cap 3.3%	US Small Cap 1.3%	Cdn Bonds 4.1%	US Small Cap -16.5%

Source: Globe HySales December 2007

Canadian Bonds: DEX Universe Bond Total Return Index
Canadian Large Cap: S&P/TSX Total Return Index
Canadian Small Cap: BMO Nesbitt Burns Cdn Small Cap Index
Emerging Markets: MSCI Emerging Markets Free Index ($Cdn)
Global Equities: MSCI World Index ($Cdn)
Foreign Equities: MSCI EAFE Index ($Cdn)
US Large Cap: S&P 500 Total Return Index ($Cdn)
US Small Cap: Russell 2000 Index ($Cdn)

investment. There is usually a cost to hedge, but it may well be worth it if the Canadian dollar increases in value against another currency as quickly as it did in 2007 in relation to the U.S. dollar. Talk to your financial advisor about this.

UNDERSTAND THE SUCCESSFUL (OR NOT) INTERGENERATIONAL TRANSFER OF WEALTH

Thirty percent of boomers view taxes as the chief threat to their inheritance, according to a recent Decima Research Poll (April 2007). And, more than 70% of family-owned businesses do not survive the transition from founder to second generation. In most cases, the "killer" is taxes or family discord; both issues that good family business succession plans will cover[4].

It is important to think about what you wish your legacy to be, and how it should be passed on. For some, the transition of wealth will be resolved by making a charitable donation; for others, it is leaving money for children and grandchildren and for others, it is to enjoy life to the fullest and to not worry about what will be left over at the end. Regardless of your wishes, I have yet to find anyone that wishes to leave a lot of money to the taxman!

Canada Revenue Agency (CRA) is not shy about claiming what is due from your estate. But why not make that a smaller amount, with more money going to support people or initiatives that are dear to you? With even some basic tax planning, you can accomplish much and you can do so while legally reducing the amount that will go to CRA.

To illustrate, let's look at the following chart. In British Columbia, if your estate at the time of your death consists of the assets listed on the left hand side, you will see that the balances left in RRSPs are all taken into income on your final tax return, if you have no surviving spouse or financially dependent minor children at the time of your death. This subjects your remaining wealth to high marginal tax rates at death.

---

[4]Source: About.com: Small Business Canada (http://sbinfocanada.about.com/cs/buysellabiz/a/succession1.htm)

For the other assets, the difference between the fair market value at the time of your death and adjusted cost base of the asset (which often is the cost at time of purchase) results in a capital gain, of which $\frac{1}{2}$ is taken into income and taxed at the same high marginal tax rate. The end result is taxes payable by your estate, in this case, of $305,146. Do you really feel fine about leaving all of that to CRA?

Speak to your tax and financial advisors about the impact of taxes on the wealth you have accumulated and preserved throughout your lifetime. Much can be done to ensure that a deemed disposition of your property at death won't make the taxman your largest beneficiary.

Tax Liabilities at Death

This table provides an estimate of the tax liabilities at death assuming there is no surviving spouse. The figures are to be used for illustration purposes only as your specific situation may involve rules and legislation not addressed by this table.

Assets Owned	Fair Market Value	Adjusted Cost Base	Capital Gain	Taxable Gain @ 50.00%	Income Tax @ 46.41%
RRSPs/RRIFs	$500,000	–	–	–	$232,050
Registered Pension	$0	–	–	–	$0
Mutual Funds	$50,000	$20,000	$30,000	$15,000	$6,962
Stocks	$50,000	$20,000	$30,000	$15,000	$6,962
Bonds	$25,000	$20,000	$5,000	$2,500	$1,160
Rental real estate	$200,000	$50,000	$150,000	$75,000	$34,807
Cottage	$150,000	$50,000	$100,000	$50,000	$23,205
Totals	**$975,000**				**$305,146**

This chart is for illustrative purposes only and is not intended to calculate your actual tax liability.

Source: Ativa Concept Toolkit 9 (www.ativa.com)

IN SUMMARY

THINGS YOU NEED TO KNOW

- Real wealth is what you are left with after taxes, inflation, currency risk and the cost of generating the capital you'll have for your use in the future.
- If you can be tax efficient in earning investment income throughout your lifetime, you'll keep more in your own pocket.
- Diversifying your income sources can help—a lot.
- There is a difference in tax treatment between a registered and non-registered account.
- When you "realize" income for tax purposes—and how often you do so—can impact your real wealth over time.
- Your tax and financial advisors, working on a team approach will help you accumulate more real wealth.

QUESTIONS YOU NEED TO ASK

- At what marginal rates are my different income sources taxed?
- What should I do to diversify my income sources to help me keep more income and capital?
- Where should I invest first: into a registered or non-registered savings account?
- How do the income results from different investment vehicles impact my taxes today?
- How do I plan for an inflation-protected portfolio?
- What can I do to hedge against currency risk?
- Should I be keeping an eye on wealth transition at death—even if I am single today?

THINGS YOU NEED TO DO

- Find a tax advisor to help you plan investments with your financial advisor, if the financial advisor does not have the tax expertise.
- Take a long term approach to investing.
- Understand how tax efficiency can work as a hedge against inflation.

DECISIONS YOU NEED TO MAKE

- Decide to learn more about your tax efficient income mix.
- Decide upon the questions you need to pose to your financial advisors to ensure a tax efficient approach.
- Decide on the best time of year to calculate your projected real wealth (at least once a year) to take into account inflation, taxes and currency risk.

MASTER YOUR REAL WEALTH
What is "Real" Wealth?

TIPS

- Recognize that different types of income are taxed differently.
- Be aware of the turnover of investments in your portfolio so as to maximize tax-efficiency.
- Understand the impact inflation can have on your future purchasing power.
- Realize that when investing in foreign markets, currency fluctuations can impact on your investment returns.
- Proper estate planning is integral to the successful transfer of wealth.

TRAPS

- A higher rate of return may not offer you a better after-tax financial result.
- A 'safe' investment may not give you the purchasing power you need if inflation is higher than the return on the investment.
- Global diversification opens the world's markets to you but be aware of any currency risk that might result from holding foreign investments.
- Don't think that if you use a discount brokerage firm to process trades for you that you will reduce your costs for a non-registered account. These costs may well be offset by higher income taxes as a result of the trades you are requesting they process.

Principle Mastery: It's important to dodge the key eroders of wealth—taxes, inflation, currency risk—to keep more income today and more capital tomorrow. To do so, you need to work with a team of tax and financial advisors focused on tax efficiency, income source and frequency of taxable receipts.

CHAPTER 3

What are Your Plans?

Paradise, that's my retirement plan. UNKNOWN WISE PERSON

Susan and Tom called to set up a meeting in order to ensure they have enough money for retirement. They would like to retire now, at age 55, but decided it would be wise to have a financial professional review their finances before finalizing their plans to retire. When we met and I started to ask the normal questions about what they were going to do in retirement, where they would be living, and if they expected to have to support either adult children or aging parents in the future, it quickly became evident that they would have to take a step back and discuss their retirement plans with each other. You see, Susan was wanting to spend more time with the grandchildren who all lived in their neighbourhood but Tom had always wanted to take a motorcycle trip across North America. In fact, he thought that was what Susan wanted too when she agreed to let Tom buy bigger motorcycles for both of them.

In situations in which two people are involved, it is important to recognize that each individual may have their own ideas of what they want to accomplish—and it's not unusual that these ideas may not yet have been shared with the other person in the relationship. Sometimes it is assumed that the other person "knows what you are thinking".

THE ISSUES

How is it possible that two people living together don't share their future retirement plans? In fact, studies have shown that spouses do a terrible job of communicating their goals around such important life events.

As with anything in life, having a goal gives us a sense of purpose and keeps us motivated. So it is with a savings program. When you are in your thirties, though, the concept of retirement may not hold much value for you. After all, do you even know what you want to do in retirement? Expect the nature of your discussions with your financial professional to change as your life evolves.

Financial planning is a process that determines how you can best meet your life goals through properly managing your financial affairs. If you work with a Certified Financial Planner, he or she has a responsibility to work under an Engagement Letter (in brief, a contract outlining what is to be achieved and what each of your responsibilities are). He or she will review your entire financial situation which will include your assets and liabilities (your personal net worth statement), your income and expenses (your budget), your investments, asset allocation and risk tolerance profile, your insurance coverage (risk management) and your tax situation. You may not be requesting that a comprehensive financial plan be completed—perhaps you are only concerned with your investment portfolio and some tax planning—but since these areas are all inter-connected, some review of each is required. Expect your Certified Financial Planner to ask a lot of questions! It's an excellent opportunity to have an in-depth discussion of your future goals (and if you are a couple, each of your goals) and can help crystallize your thoughts.

Maintaining a balance between what you want to do today and what you want for the future is vital to the success of any program. For most of us, when we are deprived of something, our 'need' for that something grows larger and larger.

Similarly, each individual has different priorities and dreams/goals. Suggesting that certain lifestyle expenditures be reduced in order to achieve those goals has not proven to be useful to my clients. It is my role, however, to help him/her understand the consequences of various choices so that an informed decision can be made.

In short, mastering your real wealth is an evolutionary process of informed decision making with the assistance of your most trusted advisor. That person can help you approach and achieve your plans. However, this requires some time, thought and work from you. *Talking about these issues cannot happen two weeks before your goal is to be reached.*

THE SOLUTIONS

There are four issues to consider while going through the planning process.

- Understand what is important to you.
- Who else is impacted by the decisions you make?
- Understand what your costs will be.
- Psychological impediments to planning.

UNDERSTANDING WHAT IS IMPORTANT TO YOU

The baby boomers who are now moving into retirement have a very different outlook from their parents. While the previous generation saved their money and often benefited from a company defined benefit pension plan (a plan that lets you know how much money you will receive in retirement, with the employer assuming the risk of markets performing poorly), those retiring now are more likely to work at least part-time in retirement.

Many boomers have also had to assume much of the market risk for their retirement savings in recent times, since many of the defined benefit pension plans have been eliminated or replaced with a defined contribution pension plan (which can't predict how much you can take out until retirement and which may change if markets drop sharply).[1]

---

[1]"It is reported that between 1991 and 2004 the number of paid workers covered by a RPP (Registered Pension Plan) fell from 44.3% to 39%. At the same time, the proportion of workers covered by defined benefit pension plans is declining."
"Assuming More Responsibility", *Connecting Insights, Issue 1*, BMO Retirement Institute, BMO Finanical Group®. www.retirementyyourway.com

These hard financial realities will affect your plans for the future. So can different views of how to spend your precious resources of time and money by the people you love. You may be the type of individual who loves to travel but have not had the time to do so. Your first priority in retirement, therefore, is to get to see the world. On the other hand, if you have travelled extensively for business, another plane trip may be the last thing you want to take on once you have finished working. You may be an avid sailor or your grandchildren may be the most important thing in your life. Each person has their own priorities and the challenge can be when these are different for each member within a committed relationship. The following are just some examples of what your goals might be:

- Acquiring a vacation property
- Ensuring your disabled child/grandchild is adequately taken care of
- Reducing income taxes—now and in the future
- Leaving a legacy—to family or a charity
- Paying off your debt (including that 40 year mortgage you took out 10 years before retirement)
- Making sure you can cover the costs of long-term care should that be needed

When you take the time to understand what is important to you and your loved ones, write it down, and discuss it, you and your advisors can do a better job of planning the finances you need to make your plans a reality.

UNDERSTAND WHO ELSE IS IMPACTED BY THE DECISIONS YOU MAKE

As someone who specializes in the retirement planning field, one of the questions I always ask clients at the initial fact-finding meeting is "what are your plans for retirement?" It is not uncommon for that to be the first time the clients, as a couple, have verbalized their plans. Can you imagine the dilemma when they realize that George wants to go fishing and Mary wants to travel? There is nothing wrong with having different interests but learning this one year before retirement may be too late. If George is the financial decision maker and his goal in retirement is to relax, fish and shoot the breeze with his buddies, their financial resources might just be enough to let that take place. But what is Mary going to do? She has friends that want to travel but does she have money to do so?

Similarly, you may find that your adult children would prefer you move across the country so that you can be close to the grandchildren (and to help baby-sit) but you want to downsize and live close to friends who have moved to a wonderful retirement community on the coast. While you may have the financial resources to do either, *letting others know your plans in advance can certainly help deal with those family dynamics that always occur.*

You may also find that you and your partner have different risk tolerance levels and so, when the markets are in turmoil, an emotional reaction might well cause your partner to react and put all of your investments into cash. I believe that each partner can have a portfolio specific to their own risk tolerance (instead of portfolios which are identical in makeup).

Emotional decisions can in fact play havoc with your future finances. Studies have identified an interesting sequence of events and consequences:

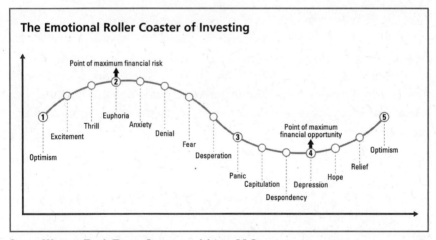

The Emotional Roller Coaster of Investing

Point of maximum financial risk

Optimism
Excitement
Thrill
Euphoria
Anxiety
Denial
Fear
Desperation
Panic
Capitulation
Despondency
Depression
Hope
Relief
Optimism

Point of maximum financial opportunity

Source: Westcore Funds/Denver Investment Advisors LLC

As the market rises, investors are optimistic (1) and begin participating in it. At the peak, euphoria (2) reins, with investors believing the market can only continue to rise. As the market drops (3), investors start panicking and at the bottom (4), investors are too scared to make further stock purchases—at a time when stocks are "on sale". Once the market rises again, investors jump back in but may already have missed the best returns of the market (see chapter 4, page 54).

Emotional reactions to decision making affect family income and inter-generational wealth. Think about this before a crisis hits. How will you react when markets rise and fall, your health fails or other stressful events occur—death or divorce for example? *Family discussions in advance will give each of you an opportunity to understand how to make better decisions about your real wealth, all of which will impact your future planning efforts.*

UNDERSTAND WHAT YOUR COSTS WILL BE

Many news stories have been written about the cost of mutual funds and how much more Canadians pay for their mutual funds than in the U.S. What is not talked about, though, is that in the U.S. many financial professionals collect an "advisor fee" over and above the management fee charged by the fund companies. The combination of the two is often close to what Canadian fund companies charge for their mutual fund products.

Like all professionals, your financial professional is entitled to earn an income for the service(s) they provide to you. The cost of working in the financial services industry is also increasing incrementally each year and such costs are assumed by your advisor in order to offer you a variety of products and services. Whether or not he or she is adequately or over-compensated is something you need to ask yourself—and perhaps your financial professional.

If your advisor offers to sell you a financial product, you should know he or she will be paid a commission or fee. Individual stocks and bonds and other securities such as exchange-traded funds (ETFs) are sold with a trading fee. Mutual funds can be sold in a variety of ways either by paying your advisor an amount up front or by a variety of deferred charges. That means you don't pay anything at the outset but if you decide to cash in your investments earlier than outlined in the original schedule, you will pay a fee. Advisors are also compensated for ongoing service to the client by way of "trailer fees", which are higher if the funds have not been sold on a deferred sales charge basis, because the advisor will not have received compensation at the time of the initial sale. Most insurance products pay much of the overall compensation to the advisor at the time of sale, with a small annual residual paid out thereafter for ongoing servicing of the client.

It is important to note that all individuals selling mutual funds, securities, insurance and similar products do so through an intermediary (a dealership, securities firm, insurance managing general agency) which, in return for facilitating the transactions and providing a compliance or underwriting service, receive a portion of the advisor's compensation.

What you need to understand is how your advisor is paid and how that impacts on your investments. You also need to understand what your advisor does for you and how to extract value from your relationship to build and grow your real wealth.

If your advisor only sells you the financial product and then you never hear from her or him again until the next time they want to sell you something, you may wish to have some sort of discussion with your advisor about the compensation being received and its correlation to services rendered. If your advisor also offers you financial planning advice, which can include tax and estate planning, retirement planning, asset allocation, etc., you may well be receiving good value for the money being paid to the advisor by way of the trailer fees and which come out of the fund's management expense ratio. And if the advisor is proactive and offers regular consolidated portfolio statements, portfolio and insurance reviews, education opportunities and a host of other services and continually upgrades his or her own education, you are probably working with someone who understands his or her role to be one of a professional advisor and who is interested in working with clients over the long-term.

In short, much as there are a myriad of financial products and services available today, there are a variety of ways in which your financial advisor can be compensated. Some offer their services on an hourly basis, others by commission sales or as a percentage of assets they are managing and still others by a combination of all three. While it's true that most advisors these days are much more comfortable discussing how they get paid, the consumer should feel free to ask about that if the subject is not raised. And if there is a way to make that payment more tax effective for you, as can be done in some instances with non-registered monies, why not avail yourself of that option if it can be offered? Just recognize that knowing your costs is different from knowing what your financial professional earns from the products and services he or she provides.

A discussion of compensation is always appropriate even if you feel you are being well served by your financial professional.

UNDERSTAND THE PSYCHOLOGICAL IMPEDIMENTS TO PLANNING

It's okay to know that some planning for your future is needed, even if you just can't quite get around to it. What you need to look at, though, is why is this so difficult for you? Planning need not be a tedious, time-consuming task. In fact, sometimes the simpler the process, the better it is. And, you should know, there is no one best way to plan. Everyone has different reasons to put it off; what is required is coping strategies to make it happen.

Time at a Premium

You may be one of those individuals that fall into the "sandwich generation"—your adult children have come home with their family and you are taking care of an aging parent. Time is at a premium and I know there is not one minute more in your day to add anything to it.

If the task seems big, make it small. Take one action. Have your financial professional review your insurance arrangements so that at least the wealth you are building is protected. Or, call your advisor and ask if the asset allocation for your investments is the best for you at this time and if not, what recommendations can he/she make?

Once you have started, you will most likely build some momentum, so write down the other questions or concerns that you think of and schedule them for review at periodic intervals. Perhaps your financial professional can advise which should be a priority and can help you set a schedule of reviews that are manageable and efficient. Get those dates into your calendar.

The Ostrich Syndrome

You may be hesitant about what the planning will uncover. Maybe you can't retire at age 55 after all. Or, you know that with your current debt load, the result of helping your children pay for their education, retirement seems like a distant dream.

My experience as a financial planner is that, if you are open to new ideas and are flexible, some solution can usually be found. Yes, plans may have to be modified but the sooner you are able to make adjustments, the less those plans need to change. When you take the time to look up and face the music, it may be sweeter than you think. Your planner can help you approach the reality of diminished finances with a plan for accumulation and growth of new funds.

Mother Made Me Do It

A lot of our attitudes and anxieties toward money were likely developed when we were growing up. If your parents each had different attitudes toward money resulting in conflict, you may become tense when approaching financial matters. Childhood is also a time for shaping self-esteem, another predictor of our relationship with money.

In a study published by the *Journal of Family and Consumer Services* in 1999, Dr. Tahira Hira of Iowa State University and Olive Mugenda of Kenyatta University found a strong correlation between an individual's sense of self-worth and their financial habits. Overspending is seen far more frequently in people with low self-esteem. Money is not used just to meet obvious and practical needs but also to meet many socio-psychological needs.

Knowing something about why and how you react to different financial situations can help you work through such issues and make progress in working through the planning process.

Mastering Your Real Wealth is being purposeful about your goals, and achieving the financial peace of mind to make them happen.

IN SUMMARY

THINGS YOU NEED TO KNOW

- Financial planning can help you meet your goals and maintain balance between what you want to do today and what you can do in the future.
- Your choices have consequences, for you and for your family members.
- To Master Your Real Wealth you need to embark on a process to make informed decisions.

QUESTIONS YOU NEED TO ASK

- What are my priorities for the future?
- Are those priorities aligned with those I am closest to?
- Who will be impacted by the decisions I make?
- Have I let my loved ones know what I want to do?
- What is my risk tolerance level for volatility in my personal and financial affairs?
- What are the costs of working with a financial advisor to help me?
- What are the impediments I have to working in a wealth management process?

THINGS YOU NEED TO DO

- Have a family meeting to discuss your goals for the future.
- Take a short term and a long term approach to financial planning.
- Involve a professional advisory team to get the most value for your precious time and money.

DECISIONS YOU NEED TO MAKE

- Do one thing: when time is at a premium, take one action to mitigate risk.

- Get started: even if your financial situation is not in great shape. Time is money, the sooner you start the better your chances of growing your pot of gold.

- Money and self esteem are linked. Understand your relationship with money and how to integrate it in the planning process.

MASTER YOUR REAL WEALTH
What are Your Plans?

TIPS

- Goals give us a reason to stick to a program.
- Decide what is important to you at this time in your life.
- Make plans together with the other important people in your life.
- Understand how your professionals get paid so you can determine if you are getting value for your money.
- Write down questions as you think of them, so that you may periodically review them with your advisor when you can.
- Financial plans need to be modified occasionally; don't wait—the sooner you do it, the less your life plans may need to change.
- Recognize the obstacles that get in the way of your planning so you can move forward.

TRAPS

- Don't think no one else cares about your future plans; in fact, they might have some very specific views about your plans. Better to find out early enough In order to be able to make adjustments if necessary.
- Don't assume your financial professional is over-paid. Focus on the value you are extracting from your relationship.

Principle Mastery: Mastering Your Real Wealth starts with knowing yourself and your plans for the future, how that interacts with those of your significant relationships and how you can use professional help to accumulate, grow, preserve and transition the financial resources you need to make your goals happen.

CHAPTER 4

Managing Vices:
Fear and Greed

It's not the man who has too little, but the man who craves more, who is poor.
SOURCE UNKNOWN

Martin had purchased 10,000 shares of XYZ Inc. at a price of $1.10/share just prior to the company's initial public offering. During the first week of the stock being publicly listed, the share price went to $15/share and Martin was ecstatic. He immediately purchased another 100 shares; certain these too would continue to go up in price.

After the third week, there were some negative rumblings in the press about the product that XYZ Inc. had just brought to the market. Apparently some risks of injury were associated with the product during the trial process but this was never disclosed. The stock dropped to $5/share on that news.

During the ensuing months, the stock continued to drop and eventually settled at $3/share. A friend of Martin's said that perhaps he should sell those shares and invest in something else. After all, even if XYZ Inc. shares were to rise again to $15/share, it would take a very long time. In the meantime, he could deploy what money he had left and hopefully recapture some of that growth much more quickly. Martin would not hear of it: he was not going to sell his stock at a loss.

THE ISSUES

Is Martin correct in wanting to wait until his shares return to their original value before selling them?

We often have poorly understood emotions attached to our financial assets—emotions that as a financial planner I need to understand in order to encourage my client to do what is in his or her best long-term interests. Fear and greed can have a negative impact on real wealth because they are emotional reactions to situations that require rational thinking.

Martin feels the regret of buying additional shares of XYZ Inc. and feels so strongly that he doesn't want to record a loss that he ignores the fact that he may recover his loss quicker by moving what is left of XYZ Inc. into another investment. If XYZ Inc. will not recover its value for another year but another investment will grow significantly over the same time period, Martin will actually be better off by making a change in investments now. He needs to let go of his regret about the loss and work towards maximizing his financial assets by acting now.

In managing our fear and greed, there are four issues to consider.

- The psychology of investing.
- Your financial personality.
- Your financial goals and their role in your future.
- The role of your financial professional.

THE PSYCHOLOGY OF INVESTING

Money has considerable power in our lives. It determines what we eat, how we live, what car we drive, our clothes, our leisure activities and much more. Money itself has no value—other than the value we as a society attach to it. As a result, our relationship with money can be as emotional as any other relationship.

Our life experiences also influence our emotions about money. Those born in the 1920s experienced the depression and as a result, were careful when spending their money. Boomers, in general, grew up in a comfortable lifestyle but with a changing job market, easy credit, high taxation and now, at the back end, looming threats to life savings and social programs. Consequently they developed a more "live in the moment" attitude and thought nothing of borrowing to enjoy their lifestyle.

The subsequent generation of individuals began their careers in a global economy, and most recently, much tougher economic times. They have suffered a round of job losses early, and are not always earning the same level of incomes as their parents were able to at various life stages. As a result, they have not developed the same loyalty to their employers as previous generations did and having a balance between leisure and work is of paramount importance to them. They have also often missed the opportunity to tap into vested employer sponsored pension plans at a younger age. This should be of concern, but may not be.

The important thing to realize is that your feelings or emotions affect your behaviour and your decisions about money, no matter what generation you fall into. Further, those intergenerational differences can impact family wealth accumulation activities.

As markets become more volatile—whether they are at a high or a low—investors become more emotional. As discussed in the previous chapter, at the front end of a market cycle, when an investment gains value, the investor becomes more excited. Eventually, euphoria overcomes judgement and at the point of maximum risk, the investor chooses to increase his/her position in a security. At the other end of the market cycle, however, where we see the point of maximum financial opportunity, the investor's confidence in the market hits an all time low and the security is sold. In the absence of a definitive planning process, that encompasses a holistic approach to the long term destroyers of wealth, including taxes, investment cost and inflation, it is difficult to master your real wealth and the emotions attached to accumulating, growing and preserving it.

Behavioural finance research has found the following:[1]

- People default to what they know. For instance, they may extrapolate on recent trends or fixate on some old information. This can lead to a reluctance to purchase a stock or reinforce the inclination to sell a stock trading at a 52-week high.

---

[1]Source: Fiduciary Trust of Canada: When Emotions Run High

- People have a propensity to keep losers and sell winners. This can be attributed to feelings of regret, anger or disappointment when faced with selling the investment.

- People compartmentalize assets for downside protection and those for upside potential, rather than seeing the strengths and weaknesses of their whole portfolio.

- Most investors tend to think they have a much greater ability to forecast inherently unpredictable events than is actually the case.

The cost of letting your emotions drive your investment decisions is higher than you may think. It is a fact that a disciplined investor will accumulate significantly more wealth than an emotional investor.

One way to look at this is to consider the impact of missing the best days in the market by pulling out in times of market crisis and re-investing when the market appears to be calmer. The following chart clearly shows how staying invested, and not reacting to your emotions, can pay off.

JUMPING IN AND OUT OF THE MARKET MAY COST YOU[2]

S&P/TSX TR—10 Years Ended December 31, 2007

	Average Annual Return	Value of $10,000
Fully Invested	9.47%	$24,720
Missed 10 Best Days	5.26%	$16,660
Missed 20 Best Days	1.91%	$12,061
Missed 30 Best Days	-0.96%	$9,090
Missed 40 Best Days	-3.35%	$7,154
Missed 50 Best Days	-5.48%	$5,755
Missed 60 Best Days	-7.43%	$4,706

This table is for illustrative purposes only and is based on investing $10,000 for a period of 10 years ending Dec. 31/07. The indicated rates of return are historical annual compounded total returns including changes in share/unit value and reinvestment of all dividends/distributions and do not take into account sales, redemption, distribution or optional charges or income taxes payable by any security holder that would have reduced returns.

Controlling our reactions to market changes is critical if we wish to reach our goals. Remember that your plan was developed using certain long-term assumptions; knee-jerk reactions have no place in the planning process.

---

[2]Source: Franklin Templeton "5 Things You Need to Know to Ride out a Volatile Stock Market"

It's normal for all investors to question whether or not staying the course is the correct thing to do. At times, making a change is appropriate because the assumptions made at the outset are no longer valid. Things change. But we must also remember that there may be other costs associated with such change—perhaps taxes or trading fees. It's important to assess whether or not there is a structural change that needs to be accommodated in your portfolio or if there is a hiccup in the market that shall soon pass.

Sometimes doing nothing is the best thing you can do. If you work with a financial professional, having a discussion with him or her about your concerns is always appropriate. If nothing else a trained professional, whose job it is to manage wealth for others, can help you keep your emotions in check.

YOUR FINANCIAL PERSONALITY

The financial services industry is full of terms for different investor types, different retiree styles, money personalities and risk levels. At the end of the day, in order to be comfortable with the structure of your investment portfolio and its performance over the long term, you need to really understand what level of risk you are prepared to take during different lifecycles.

Understanding Your Relationship with Risk and Reward

There are a variety of tools to help financial advisors try to gauge that—and my experience is that those tools are a good starting point but one never really knows one's true risk tolerance level until it has been tested. As a result, I will often make recommendations that are somewhat more conservative than what I ascertain the client's risk level to be.

How can you determine how much risk you can tolerate so you don't get caught on that emotional rollercoaster and react in a way that is detrimental to your long term investment goals? Choosing the right investment products to meet your strategy and goals is important. This begins with a discussion about your values and your tolerance for risk.

What is your vision for investing and your value system for dealing with events that may be beyond your control? When you know your vision and values, you can have a better discussion about risk aversion and reaction to volatility, and make better decisions in both good times and more turbulent times.

Let's look at this in relatively simple terms. How would you rate your risk tolerance level?

1. You are completely **risk averse**. ANY loss will be devastating for you, either on financial or emotional terms.
2. You have a **need for income** on a regular basis and that is more important to you than the future growth of your investments.
3. You have or will soon **need income** on a regular basis **but some growth** is needed for your future.
4. You have a **long time horizon** (more than 10 years) before you will need to draw on your investment portfolio.
5. You have **extra money** that you would like to grow but you will not suffer financially if you should lose some or all the value of the investment.

It is important to discuss these five points in detail with your life partners and your financial advisors to better establish your vision and values for investing, and your risk tolerance level. This will help you put a plan in place for both fear and greed when both emotions threaten your desired outcomes.

Investment Product Selection is Important

Next, we need to understand the different types of investment vehicles there are to choose from to match vision, values and risk tolerance levels. The following are some common choices.

- Savings Accounts/GICs/Money Market Funds
- Canadian Common Stocks, Canadian Mutual Funds/ETFs/Index Funds
- Preferred Shares, Bonds
- International or Global Mutual Funds/ETFs/Index Funds

Most of these investments can generally be held inside or outside a registered account.

What is the role of each investment type in a tax efficient investment income or capital accumulation plan? What is the role of each type of investment in a tax-efficient estate plan? What risk tolerance level do we attach to each in the short term and the long term? Which do we invest in first or last to meet our goals?

To answer some of these questions involves an inter-advisory approach between your tax and financial advisors. However, it also involves the realization, in your investment selection plan, that there is the risk of not taking enough risk. Look at the following calculation.

The Risk of Not Taking a Risk

Keeping your money safe in "no risk" investments such as bank accounts, GICs and Canada Savings Bonds may keep your money safe but it may increase your exposure to the risk of not having enough money to meet your retirement needs. With "safe" investments there is a risk of having a very low or even negative rate of return because of taxes and inflation. By including some investments with higher returns and longer term growth potential in your portfolio, you reduce the risk of an income shortage during retirement.

"No Risk" Investments	
Rate of return	4.00%
Less taxes*	-1.74%
Less inflation	-2.00%
Real return	0.26%

*at a 43.41% marginal tax rate

Can a real return of 0.26% provide you with enough growth to meet your future needs?

Source: Ativa Concept Toolkit 9 (www.ativa.com)

Once you have understood that there can be a risk in being too conservative in your investment approach, it is somewhat easier to determine your risk tolerance level.

Asset Allocation

Along with understanding how much risk you can withstand, is the subject of asset allocation. This involves not only the selection of assets to be held in your portfolio but also in what percentage of the portfolio each asset type will fit. We do this to properly factor each asset type into the portfolio's risk profile and determine whether or not it is suitable for your risk tolerance level.

The following matrix is a very basic asset allocation chart which can serve as a basis for determining an asset allocation for your portfolio or to use as a point of discussion with your advisor.

Investor Type	Suggested Asset Components
Risk Averse and Understands the Risk This May Pose	Savings Accounts/GICs/Money Market Funds
Needs Income	Savings Accounts/GICs/Money Market Funds Preferred Shares, Bonds
Needs Income With Some Growth	Savings Accounts/GICs/Money Market Funds Preferred Shares, Bonds Canadian Common Stocks/Mutual Funds/ETFs/Index Funds
Long Time Horizon	Preferred Shares, Bonds Canadian Common Stocks/Mutual Funds/ETFs/Index Funds International or Global Mutual Funds/ETFs/Index Funds
Extra Money	Canadian Common Stocks/Mutual Funds/ETFs/Index Funds International or Global Mutual Funds/ETFs/Index Funds

Now I don't for one minute want you to think that this is all there is to know about putting your portfolio together—because it's not. It is quite a complex subject and there is some art and some science in putting together a portfolio you can be comfortable with. It is simply a starting point for you to be able to ask the correct questions about what sort of investments might be suitable for you. But remember, just because a certain asset class may generate a higher return, does not mean that it is appropriate for you. Risk and return are trade-offs; know how much of each you are comfortable with.

Mastering your real wealth also requires you to look at your investment selections with an after-tax and inflation-adjusted viewpoint, with an eye on the costs of investing. All of this must be discussed with your advisory team to understand your true risks and rewards.

YOUR FINANCIAL GOALS AND THEIR ROLE IN YOUR FUTURE

It's time to go back to why Real Wealth Management™ is important to you. Consider that at any point in time you are moving towards a certain life stage and your savings are being built for that purpose. How do you see that unfolding? What goals do you need to set to manage financial outcomes in both the short term and the long term? It is often helpful to take a strategic look at the purpose behind your goals in advance of various lifecycles.

Starting a Family

If this is the time to start your family, how many children does that mean? Remember that there is a cost to having children, including the increasing costs of their post-secondary education. However, if everyone thought about all the costs of having children beforehand, they would never have them, so I don't want you to get lost in the details! But if education will be important, consider whether you can start a savings program for that purpose early in your children's lives to make the expense more manageable for you? Fortunately there are a number of tax-advantaged ways for you to do so, opportunities that should be discussed with your advisors.

Buying a House

Now it's time to buy a house. What is important to you and what are you willing to give up? If you want a single family house and some yard around it, are you willing to commute in order to have that? On the other hand, if you are always in a certain area for your leisure time, does it make more sense (financial or otherwise) to live close to work or your leisure-time location? Owning a principal residence has significant wealth accumulation and preservation benefits, and tax efficiencies.

Upgrading your Education

Your career is moving along nicely but it would be better for you in the long run if you upgraded your education. Can you study part-time, by correspondence or must you attend a university or college on a full-time basis? Will returning to school increase your future income or are you doing this to improve your job satisfaction—or both?

Next consider which financial "bucket" you will need to tap into to do so? Is there a tax advantaged way to do so? For example, do you want to withdraw some of your RRSPs tax free under the Lifelong Learning Plan or will you save additional money for this education? Do you have money in a Tax-Free Savings Account for these purposes? Can new programs under Employment Insurance help? Or is your employer willing to put you through school, providing you with a potential tax free perk?

Getting Ready for Retirement

Your children are getting older and you want to start thinking about retirement. What does retirement mean to you? Where will you be living? What will you be doing? Do you know how much money you will need to live the life you are choosing? How will your extended families fit into the picture? Will you need to help an aging parent, financially or otherwise? What effect do those questions have on your finances? Where will the money come from to meet all the demands your extended family may have of you? When is the right time to ask these questions?

In Retirement

You are in retirement and starting to feel some of the aches and pains of getting older. Will your healthcare costs be covered under an insurance plan? Do you think you may need to go into a long-term care facility or are you adamant that you want to continue to live at home, no matter what? Have you thought about what sort of legacy you would like to leave? Are you concerned about tax erosion of your estate upon death?

Obviously, there are events unique to you that need to be addressed both in family meetings, and also in meetings with your professional advisory team. Planning ahead need not be anxiety ridden—in fact, setting strategies and goals will allow you to consider options in your decision making and if there is something you don't like about those options, you have the time to prepare or try to change course if you need to.

Planning with defined goals also helps you to understand the level of risk that you can or are prepared to take during a specific life phase. For instance, if you are saving to buy a house in the next few years, you will want to ensure the money you need will be available to you at that time. It may not be appropriate to take more risk for that specific investment pool. On the other hand, your retirement may be a long way off so you might be prepared to take a bit more risk in order to reap the potential of higher returns. Balancing the timeline with the investment needs will help to ensure you don't become swayed by higher returns offered elsewhere.

THE ROLE OF YOUR PROFESSIONAL FINANCIAL ADVISOR

One of the most important services your financial professional can offer you is the rational thinking that is needed in volatile markets. He or she can be that calm port in a storm.

It's not that the professional advisor is not concerned with what is happening on the emotional front. But for the most part, he or she has more information available to gauge the situation and has the benefit of speaking with many of the money managers that are "in the field". In the investment business, there are almost limitless distractions and short-term noise. These must be kept in perspective.

As well, a financial professional can work with you to help you determine your risk profile. It's not uncommon for people to think they can tolerate more risk than they actually feel comfortable with. That little extra return may be pulling at us... but is it really necessary to take that added risk?

Even if you want to do most of the research yourself, perhaps to save costs, it can be a good idea to spend a bit of money upfront to meet with a professional to get some advice. As a financial planner, I have seen a multitude of financial situations and have worked with many clients to prepare for retirement and other life events. There are always new situations but there are lots of scenarios I may be able to advise you on, based on the experiences I have encountered.

For instance, I know that if you wish to take some increased risk with a portion of your investments, doing so in your Registered Retirement Savings Plan (RRSP) may not be appropriate. Losses within an RRSP cannot be offset against any other capital gains you may have. Therefore, if you are taking more risk—which means a greater chance of a higher return or a loss, you would be best to do so outside of your RRSP so that you can take advantage of some of the tax planning opportunities available to you.

If you don't have a pension plan, the correct asset allocation is even more important. This may entail looking not just at asset allocation but also product allocation.

You may own a business which entails significant investment and risk. Many of your eggs may be in that basket. It may not be appropriate to also take a risk with your savings.

These are just a few of the issues that will need addressing and you can choose to do a lot of the work yourself but in my opinion, you are being penny-wise, pound-foolish not to at least consult someone with experience and knowledge in this area. You may also be able to arrange a collaborative approach, if you are more comfortable with that; that is, an arrangement in which both you and the financial professional share the work, with the financial professional providing information to you in areas you are not comfortable working in. There are usually options available to you which will suit your preferred involvement level.

The emotions of fear and greed can be better managed to your long term advantage by employing strategy, a process for goal setting and the ongoing management of required decision making in collaboration with an informed team. A great way to leverage your personality, values, and game plan to manage the unexpected is with the support of additional brainpower, experience and time that a professional can add to help you achieve real wealth.

IN SUMMARY

THINGS YOU NEED TO KNOW

- Emotional decision making can significantly influence long term investment performance results.
- Money has power—this can be controlled to your advantage with strategy and process.
- Different values characterize different generations in the family; those values must be discussed and balanced in developing a Real Wealth Management™ plan.
- You can't know it all—investment product selections, asset allocation, taxation and lifestyle needs all involve technical knowledge that must be updated continuously. A knowledgeable professional team can help.

QUESTIONS YOU NEED TO ASK

- What goals do I have for my current lifecycle?
- What goals do I need to set for the future?
- What is my risk tolerance level?
- How does that match my partner's?
- What investment products are best for us?
- How does asset allocation help us tolerate risk and avoid the foibles of greed?
- How do taxes and investment costs affect the decisions we make in reacting to the unexpected?

THINGS YOU NEED TO DO

- Understand your personality and expectations relating to risk and reward.
- Know what your individual and family vision and values are when it comes to using income and building capital.

DECISIONS YOU NEED TO MAKE

- Find a team of professional advisors who really understand you (and your family) and can help fill in the technical expertise you need to make your financial dreams a reality.
- Let those professionals guide you through good times and bad.

MASTER YOUR REAL WEALTH
Managing Vices: Fear and Greed

TIPS

- Understand your relationship with money and how that affects your planning process.
- Determine what level of risk you are comfortable with to avoid putting yourself on an emotional roller coaster.
- Visualize your future to better establish your goals. Act as if you are in that moment now.
- Consider hiring a financial professional for the aspects of your plans where you have little expertise.

TRAPS

- People fixate on old information, extrapolate recent trends, have a propensity to keeps losers and sell winners, and think they have a much greater ability to forecast unpredictable events than is the case.
- Don't let a previous unsatisfactory experience with a financial professional prevent you from asking advice.
- Your emotions can wreak havoc with your financial results: remember to think first and act later.
- Understand there can be a risk of not taking a risk.
- The absence of strategy and process will result in knee jerk reactions.

Principle Mastery: Remember, managing the emotion of greed is as important as managing fear in mastering your real wealth. Goal-setting by envisioning your future is an important part of mastering your real wealth. Working with advisors who really understand you can guide you from emotional investing to disciplined decision making in good times and bad.

CHAPTER 5

Taking Stock–
Your Personal Net Worth Statement

I now have the gloomy prospect of retiring from office loaded with serious debts, which will materially affect the tranquility of my retirement.
THOMAS JEFFERSON

Fran, a single mother of two, has been fortunate in being able to build her career to the point where she is now earning $250,000/year. It does require her to work a lot of overtime but she enjoys her work and her children are now at the age where they are fairly independent. So now that Fran has fewer parental obligations, she would like to take some nice vacations. But she never seems to have enough money. She assumes it's because she pays so much in taxes, but isn't completely sure. Perhaps she is spending too much but she doesn't know where to cut back. Fran has never made up a budget except in the first few years after her divorce. In fact, after speaking with her financial advisor, she is coming to realize that not tracking where money is going is the one of the quickest ways to lose control of your finances.

THE ISSUES

It's very difficult for any of us to have the time to review our financial situation in detail, and to do so regularly. Getting copies of all the statements, knowing what is needed, understanding the information can all be overwhelming.

As with any undertaking, however, you need a starting point from which to make your plans in order to reach your destination. If you don't know where you are today, how do you know what will help you achieve your goals for tomorrow?

When Fran earns $250,000 a year, it's easy to assume she must have some extra money available to take annual vacations. She is correct in that she is probably paying a lot in income taxes (maybe she could pay less with some planning) but it's not uncommon to find that cash flow is being allocated inappropriately, perhaps to achieve one goal but at the detriment of reaching the other goals.

One example is the single mother who was using a universal life insurance policy (an insurance product with an investment component) to save for her child's education. Now there is nothing wrong with such a product but in this situation, all her cash flow was going into the policy and she was having to draw on her line of credit to pay for her other expenses. She was also foregoing the opportunity to leverage her investment with grant money from the government. By not investing in a Registered Education Savings Plan, she was not adding the Canada Education Savings Grant to the pot.

Another example is the client who was continually buying real estate for investment purposes. She kept buying more in order to trigger losses from one property to offset gains against another property. Yet this client did not own her own home—one of the most tax efficient investments she could have. That is, gains on the disposition of a home designated as the principal residence are completely tax exempt.

Putting the facts on paper can help you understand the situation in a way "keeping it in your head" never will. It can also help you add tax efficiency to the mix of investment options you have, something that can help you increase your real wealth over time.

THE SOLUTIONS

There are four major issues to understand when reviewing your financial situation:

- Your Personal Net Worth Statement.
- How Asset Acquisitions Impact Real Wealth.
- Cash Flow Versus After-Tax Income.
- The Risk Present In Your Net Worth.

YOUR PERSONAL NET WORTH STATEMENT

Your Personal Net Worth Statement is a snapshot of your current financial position. To be useful, your cash flow needs to be looked at in conjunction with your Personal Net Worth Statement and while this can be a separate document, in this book we will put the two together so you have only one document you need to work with. The example at the end of this chapter can be changed for your own situation but its format is a good starting point.

Let's look at Fran's assets, liabilities, income and expenses.

Fran's Personal Statement of Net Worth

ASSETS (LIQUID)

Cash on hand	$1,000	
Savings Accounts	$5,000	Used for annual expenses such as property taxes
Chequing Accounts	$2,000	
Cashable GICs	$5,000	Fran's emergency fund
Savings Bonds		
Other		
	$13,000	

ASSETS (SEMI-LIQUID)

Stocks		
Bonds		
Life Insurance (Cash Value)		
Mutual Funds	$50,000	If sold, these may trigger a capital gain
Term Deposits/GICs		
Annuities		
RRSP/RPP/RRIF	$300,000	
RESP	$40,000	For Fran's childrens' schooling
Other		
	$390,000	

ASSETS (NON-LIQUID)

Principal Residence (MV)	$750,000	Purchased five years ago for $500,000
Other Real Estate (MV)		
*Vehicles	$25,000	Purchased last year under a lease
Locked-in RRSP		
Deferred Compensation		
Business Interests		
*Personal/Household Effects	$150,000	Fran has recently started to collect antiques
Other		
	$925,000	

TOTALS	**$1,328,000**	

*Depreciating Assets

LIABILITIES (SHORT TERM)

*Credit Cards		
HBP (Home Buyers' Plan)	$20,000	Taken out five years ago to help buy her home
*Personal Loans	$25,000	Used to help with cash flow shortfalls
Investment Loans		
Other		
	$45,000	

LIABILITIES (LONG TERM)

Mortgage (Residence)	$150,000	Fran has repaid this rapidly—the interest rate is currently at 4%
Mortgage (Other)		
Life Insurance Policy Loan		
Other (e.g. Business, etc.)		
	$150,000	

TOTALS	**$195,000**	

*Co-Signed Loans		
*Guaranteed Loans		

*Detract from net worth

MONTHLY INCOME

Salary (After Taxes and Deductions)	$13,225	
Commissions		
Contracts		
Bonuses		
Child Support	$2,000	This is the last year she will receive this
Spousal Support		
Interest Income		
Taxable Investment Income		
Rental Income		
Student Loan Income		
Other		

TOTALS	**$15,225**	

MONTHLY EXPENSES

Rent/Mortgage	$1,812	Fran pays weekly + additional payments
Utilities (Electricity/Heat)	$200	
Day-Care Services/Babysitting		
*Cable TV/Special Channels	$200	Fran's children love all the cable channels
*Service Contracts (e.g. Cleaning, Lawn Mowing)	$10	
*Monthly Savings		
*Car Loan Payments		
RRSP Contributions	$1,665	Fran contributes the maximum each year
Child and/or Spousal Support		
*Vacation/Gift Fund		
RESP Contributions		
Personal Income Taxes (Not Deducted at Source)		
Municipal Taxes (If Not Included in Mortgage Payment)	$165	
Insurance Premiums		
*Telephone (Cell & Other)	$150	This is for 3 cell phones
Car Maintenance & Repairs		
Parking/Public Transportation	$50	Fran often has business meetings downtown
Groceries	$200	
*Entertainment (Including Dining Out)	$200	Because Fran is so busy, they often eat out
*Clothing	$400	Fran and the children all love clothes
Home Maintenance/Repairs	$100	
Household Items/Furniture	$200	This is for the antiques Fran collects
Prescriptions/Dental Work		
*Recreation (Including Newspapers/Magazines/ Movies/Club Fees)	$100	
Vet Fees/Pet Food		
Personal Care/Hairdresser	$150	
Donations	$100	

TOTALS $5,702

*May Be Discretionary

A quick review of the asset section of Fran's statement will reveal that most of her net worth is based on her residence—which is not uncommon. Assets can be divided into three main categories:

- liquid (those in cash or cash equivalents),
- semi-liquid (assets that can be converted into cash relatively easily but there may be some tax consequences or other factors to be considered) and
- non-liquid (assets not easily or quickly converted into cash).

How she uses those assets and when can have a big impact on her real wealth over time. At first glance several factors come to mind:

Fran has a $5,000 emergency fund which is a great start, but it is usually recommended you keep enough to cover between three and six months of expenses in such a fund. How much you save really depends on the security of your income. In Fran's case, her job is secure but her monthly expenses are just over $5,700 so these savings represent only one month of expenses—which is not adequate to protect Fran from the unexpected.

Fran has been saving outside of her RRSP, in mutual funds. While some of these assets could be liquidated to pay for lifestyle wants or needs, like a vacation, it will be important to remember there may be tax consequences in doing so and the timing of any sale should be looked at carefully. If Fran has tax loss carry forwards from previous years, the gains might be offset against those losses and the tax impact may be minimal. But Fran needs to also consider that some of these savings might be needed for emergency purposes. In that case, putting some of that money into a money market fund, which does not fluctuate in value, might be a wise move to make.

Fran has leased her vehicle which means she does not yet own it. On the liability section of the statement, she should have recorded the details of her lease. Note also, that both the vehicle and personal/household effects are depreciating assets. There is more to follow on this subject a bit later in this chapter.

On the liability side of Fran's Net Worth Statement, Fran has a Home Buyers' Plan (HBP) liability listed. Since this was money taken out of her RRSP five years ago to help with the purchase of her home, the amount should have been reduced by now because there is a requirement to repay the amount over a 15 year period beginning the second calendar year after the withdrawal. Since Fran has not started that repayment, she should have included the amount of those payments in her taxable income each year. This is a discussion point that will need to be addressed.

Fran also has a line of credit that she has been using to cover cash flow shortfalls. It may seem surprising that someone with an income of $15,225/month and expenses of $5,702/month will experience a shortfall. But Fran has been paying down as much as possible on her mortgage, thinking it is to her advantage to do so. If you consider that the mortgage interest rate is only 4% and the interest on the line of credit is most likely closer to 6%, it is actually costing her more money to use the line of credit. This is non-deductible interest on a loan that might be better used for investment purposes, which would also make the interest deductible.

In short, reviewing Fran's income and expenses on a preliminary basis, there are definitely some areas that are marked as discretionary—that is, Fran and her family can choose to reduce those expenses. So now Fran needs to make some decisions: are the monthly cable costs more important than the annual vacation—as one example. Putting this information down in black and white can be eye-opening. It is easier to make changes once you understand how your money is being allocated. But in the end, the decisions that will be made are better understood when a long term approach to income and wealth planning is taken.

HOW ASSET ACQUISITONS IMPACT REAL WEALTH

Over our lifetime, we acquire a lot of "stuff"—just ask anyone that is about to move. And while many items can be very expensive—think wide screen plasma TVs when they first came out—over a period of time, some will gain value and others will lose it. Since there will always be short-term fluctuations in asset values, you need to look at the longer term trend in assessing the fate of the value of your expenditures and particularly, your investments.

Let's look at real estate as an example. There is no question that anyone who purchased real estate in the last five years has probably seen the value of that asset increase significantly. Even though we experience declines in house prices at specific times, over the long term such an asset class will normally increase in value; but maybe not as much as you believe. Look at the following chart:

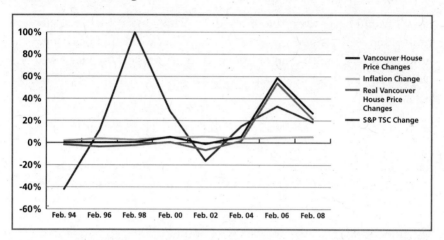

You will see that, after inflation, the 'real' change in Vancouver real estate prices did not generate growth until 2006 when the real estate market spiralled upward dramatically. And now, of course, the market has moved substantially downwards with inflation again a possible longer term concern. The after-inflation growth of real estate from 1994 to 2004 was -2.24%[1]. So why does everyone think that real estate is a great investment?

The equity you build up is mainly due to the mortgage payments you make which are a form of forced savings, after tax. And, of course, if you live in your house (instead of using it as an investment), it also provides you with shelter, a current consumption expense you need to fund. So while the growth in real estate is sometimes not as great as we all think it is, over the longer term and in most geographic areas, this asset class will generally increase or at least preserve your net worth, rather than simply eroding it. One of the reasons for this is that gains on disposition of principal residences are tax exempt. That makes your home a tax efficient investment if it goes up in value. (Not so much if it goes down—losses on personal residences are not deductible).

---

[1]Vancouver real estate prices from Feb. 1994 to 2004 increased 19.9% while inflation increased 22.14%

This is quite different from most other consumer expenditures. Consider all the new electronic toys that we love so much—or the purchase of a new car. It is very rare that either asset class will increase in value—in fact, we have seen many electronic items become significantly less expensive over time and it is rare to see a car appreciate in value the longer you hold on to it.

Now I would never say not to buy a depreciating asset—we need electronics and vehicles in our everyday lives. What we should be doing, however, if real wealth is an objective, is to determine how much we want to pay for these items, always understanding their impact on our net worth.

In Fran's case, her vehicle was purchased with a lease. So she must make monthly payments on that—payments she has not included in her expenses. This might be another reason why she feels she is "cash poor"—and is also another good reason for going through your statement of net worth.

Whether or not the lease was the wise option will depend on factors such as the cost of the lease, whether or not Fran can write off that cost and other factors that may be unique to her situation. Again, this is a discussion point that needs some consideration. Perhaps leaving the depreciation on the lot, and buying a one year old used car might have been a better plan. Has she considered how the tax consequences of these decisions affect her net worth? The help of a tax advisor would be wise.

Another issue to consider with Fran is the collection of antiques. Normally furniture items are a depreciating asset since it's not often we can sell them for more than what we paid for them. In Fran's case, the opposite is probably true. But she should check to see if she has them properly insured or after a house fire, she may only receive payment for the depreciated cost of those items. In addition, what are the tax consequences of the sale of her antiques for a profit? Again, a consultation with a tax advisor can help Fran decide how her antiques will impact her real wealth in the future.

To accumulate more real wealth, then, it is important to consider whether your after-tax dollars should be used to purchase appreciating or depreciating assets. In the former case, you may win with a tax preferred capital gain; but in the case of depreciating assets, which cannot be written off on your tax return, consider the cost carefully. Is the short term pleasure worth eroding your wealth over the long term? Could other choices, like investing in an RRSP for example, help you get what you want by leveraging your scarce dollars?

Cash Flow versus After-Tax Income

Cash flow is the money you earn; after-tax income is the money you get to keep to cover your bills. This is where the different types of income sources you earn become quite important. Not only does it make sense that you want to work in planning your affairs with the amount of money you actually keep, there are certain social benefit programs that look at your net income (line 236 of your tax return) when deciding if you are eligible for such additional cash flow. Different income sources are taxed in different ways. Different income levels will affect your eligibility for social benefits, like the Old Age Security or Child Tax Benefits. You need to understand this.

A good example is Old Age Security (OAS). Currently, OAS starts getting "clawed-back" when net income exceeds approximately $66,000. If you receive a pension of $50,000 and have non-registered investments of $300,000 earning 3% interest per annum, you will receive an additional $9,000 of income that needs to be included in your net income.

TYPE OF INCOME	$ INCOME
Pension Income	$50,000
Taxable Interest Income	$9,000
CPP	$10,600
OAS	$6,100
Total Income	$75,700

(Figures are rounded for purposes of this example).

Since any income over the OAS net income clawback threshold is subject to a claw back calculation of 15% of income[2], in this case your OAS will be reduced by close to $140/month or over $1,600/year. That is about 18% of the interest income you receive. Now if that income source being earned by the investments is changed to a "return of capital" (that is, part or all of your income from the source is structured as a return of your original capital), most of it will not be taxable with the result that more of the OAS pension falls into the taxpayer's pocket. In this case, the taxpayer would have improved annual cash flow by almost $1,400 by reducing the OAS clawback—that is, more cash flow is created, not by reducing expenditures but by reducing the amount of taxable income received.

In Fran's case, most of her income is treated as "regular" or "ordinary" income for tax purposes, causing it to be taxed at the highest marginal tax rate. There is little that Fran can do about this. But it might be in her financial interest to negotiate future raises by way of additional benefits (for instance, a longer vacation period with the vacation paid as perk of employment) instead of a higher salary. Fran should also discuss what tax free perks she can negotiate for in her next round of salary talks.

Fran also knows she will no longer be receiving the $2,000 in child support currently scheduled, but that amount is not taxable. So while there will be no change in her taxable income, she will have $2,000 less per month to cover her children's expenses. She needs to take that into account when planning for the future, and therefore income sources that provide cash flow must be considered in tandem with after-tax results to determine what Fran really has to spend each month. That's a key way that tax and financial advisors can work together in managing after-tax cash flows with their clients.

THE RISK PRESENT IN YOUR NET WORTH

There are many elements of risk that must be taken into consideration when looking at your personal net worth. Obviously, if your assets are depreciating, your net worth statement will look quite different—

---

[2] All OAS is clawed back when net income (line 236) reaches $104,903 in 2008

perhaps not far in the future—than it does today. And it won't be looking better! Your income is also required to build your net worth and that income comes in many forms. If you are prevented from earning income from employment due to illness and you are not protected by an insurance product, your net worth is not likely to grow—both because you are not able to contribute more to your savings but also because you are now drawing on those assets.

Further, if your investment income is being eroded by inflation or income taxes, again the growth of your net worth will be negatively impacted.

Increasing your debt can also very quickly erode your net worth—particularly when the capital is used to purchase a lifestyle and not an asset. An asset that provides an inflation hedge or one that is tax-efficient is the most desirable choice if your goal is wealth creation and growth.

In Fran's situation, there is no evidence of any insurance premiums being paid which begs the question of whether she has any insurance coverage. She is the sole bread winner so any loss of income will directly affect her family. As well, if she were to die, Fran's estate could have a significant tax liability, as, being single, she cannot benefit from a tax free rollover of the RRSP deposits left, particularly if her children are of legal age. (There are some opportunities for tax deferral for minor children or disabled dependants).

The remaining estate may therefore not be adequate for her children. While money has been saved for their education, most likely the amount will need to be supplemented. And the children will need to pay their own living expenses, which only add to the cost of their education—that is, unless they can be assured of staying in the house. This causes Fran to worry, yet all of those concerns can be addressed through Fran's will and early estate planning. But it doesn't happen automatically; you must be proactive.

IN SUMMARY

THINGS YOU NEED TO KNOW

- You need to keep an eye on your personal net worth to assess how wealthy you are.
- The Personal Net Worth Statement is a snapshot of your wealth as at a specific time; therefore it's a good tool in analyzing change due to market conditions or increased/decreased debt.
- Understanding how the spending choices you make will impact your real wealth is useful in your planning.
- If you want to grow real wealth over time, you need to focus on which financial choices add to your wealth and which erode your wealth.
- How taxes impact your income and capital is an extremely useful skill in building wealth. Working with your tax and financial advisor can help you understand.

QUESTIONS YOU NEED TO ASK

- What is my personal net worth?
- What are the tax consequences of my expenditures?
- When does it make sense to pay interest on a loan?
- Should I buy or rent a home in my immediate future?
- How are my different income sources taxed?
- How can I tap into more social benefits available from the government?
- Do I have enough insurance?

THINGS YOU NEED TO DO

- Set financial goals for the next one, three and five years.

- Prepare a personal net worth statement.

- Prepare a personal income and expense statement.

- Prepare a monthly and annual budget.

- Write down what you'd like to leave in your estate.

- Write down what you think you'll need to do to have security in retirement.

- Take out your tax return and find what your total taxes payable were last year. Then ask your advisors how you can reduce net and taxable income.

DECISIONS YOU NEED TO MAKE

- Have I constructed a tax efficient investment plan?

- How can I minimize taxes to increase monthly cash flow?

- Will my income and wealth management plan be at risk if I become disabled or die; how can I protect myself and my family.

MASTER YOUR REAL WEALTH
Taking Stock—Your Personal Net Worth Statement

TIPS

- Work with your advisor to use the Personal Net Worth Statement as a starting point from which to grow your wealth.
- Consider whether your assets are a hedge against inflation and taxes.
- Try to minimize your taxable income to be able to take advantage of government sponsored benefit programs and refundable and non-refundable taxes whenever possible.
- Consider whether your income is protected (insured) to provide for the future growth of your net worth.

TRAPS

- Don't get into the habit of buying 'lifestyle' assets—at least don't think this means you have increased your net worth.
- When purchasing real estate, you must be as careful of the price as you would be for any other asset. This is not a guaranteed wealth creator.
- Be aware of assets that quickly lose their value—they will not help to grow your net worth.
- Don't write insurance off as a "money grab". There is an appropriate type and amount of insurance that needs to be considered in almost every situation.

Principle Mastery: When it comes to your real wealth, it's as important to transition it to the next generation on a tax efficient basis as it is about accumulating and growing it. If you don't protect your estate from taxes or your own failing health, you will accumulate significantly less for your heirs.

Personal Net Worth Statement   Date _____

ASSETS (LIQUID)	Yours	Spouse's	Joint
Cash on hand			
Savings Accounts			
Chequing Accounts			
Cashable GICs			
Savings Bonds			
Other			

ASSETS (SEMI-LIQUID)	Yours	Spouse's	Joint
Stocks			
Bonds			
Life Insurance (Cash Value)			
Mutual Funds			
Term Deposits/GICs			
Annuities			
RRSP/RPP/RRIF			
RESP			
Other			

ASSETS (NON-LIQUID)	Yours	Spouse's	Joint
Principal Residence (MV)			
Other Real Estate (MV)			
*Vehicles			
Locked-in RRSP			
Deferred Compensation			
Business Interests			
*Personal/Household Effects			
Other			

TOTALS	Yours	Spouse's	Joint

*Depreciating Asset

Comments:

LIABILITIES (SHORT TERM)	Yours	Spouse's	Joint
*Credit Cards			
HBP (Home Buyers' Plan)			
*Personal Loans			
Investment Loans			
Other			

LIABILITIES (LONG TERM)	Yours	Spouse's	Joint
Mortgage (Residence)			
Mortgage (Other)			
Life Insurance Policy Loan			
Other (e.g. Business, etc.)			

TOTALS	Yours	Spouse's	Joint

	Yours	Spouse's	Joint
*Co-Signed Loans			
*Guaranteed Loans			

*Detract From Net Worth

Comments:

_____

MONTHLY INCOME	Yours	Spouse's	Joint
Salary (After Taxes and Deductions)			
Commissions			
Contracts			
Bonuses			
Child Support			
Spousal Support			
Interest Income			
Taxable Investment Income			
Rental Income			
Student Loan Income			
Other			

TOTALS	Yours	Spouse's	Joint

Comments:

_____

MONTHLY EXPENSES	Yours	Spouse's	Joint
Rent/Mortgage			
Utilities (Electricity/Heat)			
Day-Care Services/Babysitting			
*Cable TV/Special Channels			
*Service Contracts (e.g. Cleaning, Lawn Mowing)			
*Monthly Savings			
*Car Loan Payments			
RRSP Contributions			
Child and/or Spousal Support			
*Vacation/Gift Fund			
RESP Contributions			
Personal Income Taxesl (Not Deducted at Source)			
Municipal Taxes (If Not Included in Mortgage Payment)			
Insurance Premiums			
*Telephone (Cell & Other)			
Car Maintenance & Repairs			
Parking/Public Transportation			
Groceries			
*Entertainment (Including Dining Out)			
*Clothing			
Home Maintenance/Repairs			
Household Items/Furniture			
Prescriptions/Dental Work			
*Recreation (Including Newspapers/ Magazines/Movies/Club Fees)			
Vet Fees/Pet Food			
Personal Care/Hairdresser			
Donations			

TOTALS	Yours	Spouse's	Joint

*May Be Discretionary

Comments:

CHAPTER 6

Understanding the Process:
Income and Growth

It's better to have a permanent income than to be fascinating. OSCAR WILDE

Riki is employed with a company which has no pension plan. She has done a terrific job of saving for her retirement but with the current market volatility, she is concerned that her savings will not be sufficient in five years time when she plans to retire. She doesn't want to buy an annuity (which guarantees to pay her a specific amount of money each month) since the payout is based on current interest rates—which are very low. Riki's parents are both alive at age 90 and since she is healthy, she understands that planning for a long retirement period is essential. But she doesn't know how she can protect her income for future years. Her employer has not been able to offer her any ideas since he is struggling with how to prepare for his own retirement.

THE ISSUES

What can Riki do to protect herself in the situation she finds herself in— responsible for her income sources, both now and in retirement? She has been careful to stay as healthy as possible but has not given much thought to how to structure her retirement income using the assets within her existing investment portfolio. Neither has she given much thought to the taxes that will need to be paid when she dies and she doesn't want to burden her family with this.

There are several stages in life when receiving income will be important— for example, when building a family, in the event of illness (yours, your partner's or a family member) or at retirement—and other times when we have no choice but to draw on savings—such as a job loss or after the death of an income earning partner. You may also decide to pursue further education and this may require you to stop working for a time period.

With the wave of boomers soon to retire, the financial services industry has been introducing some very creative products to help retirees manage various retirement risks. These products can, however, be complicated and have costs associated with them so it is important to work with someone who can help you sort through the marketing pieces and find out what the real benefit is to you over the long run. Matching the right investment products to your income and capital requirements is complicated, particularly if you are taking tax efficiency into account. An additional cost for the product may well be worth the added feature(s)— for example, income for life—but the degree to which the costs erode wealth is an important question requiring a decision you should be able to make on an informed basis. Part of an informed advisor's job is to stay abreast of these product solutions and match them to your retirement plans. This relationship is important, even if you are astute in planning and managing your wealth.

Many of us feel that with some early success, we are very knowledgeable about investing, preparing our taxes, calculating how much money we need in retirement or some other aspect of financial planning. But what is often not understood is the interdisciplinary aspect of financial planning. You need someone with a wide range of financial experience and who is backed up by various specialists all of whom can work together to maximize your financial wealth.

To master the creation of income pegged for future needs is difficult because it requires numerous financial decisions along the way. If a financial professional works better with a team, would not an individual consumer do better with a team of professionals behind him or her as well?

THE SOLUTIONS

There are four distinct solutions to growing and protecting your future income which you should be aware of:

- Protecting your financial position
- Important principles in product selection
- The inheritance windfall
- Selling a business

PROTECTING YOUR FINANCIAL POSITION

As mentioned in Chapter 5, one of the most basic of financial planning rules is to ensure you have an emergency fund of savings on hand. This can mean three to six months of your income requirements, often placed in a savings account to maintain its value. If your employment is tenuous or sporadic or you are subject to layoffs, an emergency fund of more than six months is advisable. Similarly, if your employment is very secure, you may keep money in your emergency fund at the lower level but have available to you a line of credit you can draw upon if required. If you are using the line of credit for this purpose, *be sure not to draw from it unless it is an emergency.*

Prior to growing a family, if you will be living on one income instead of two after your children start to arrive, it makes sense to start living on one income in advance of that happening. Not only can this help build up some savings for the future, it helps you get disciplined about your discretionary expenses in advance. You may also want to explore how the maternity benefits under the Employment Insurance program work and what coverage your employer offers under such a situation.

In the event of an illness—and at earlier ages we are more apt to become ill than die—you will need income to continue to pay your fixed expenses as well as increased medical costs. An emergency fund is definitely required but as well, the early purchase of disability insurance or critical illness insurance can do much to protect your current assets and provide you with the income you need to be receiving while you are trying to get well. Your employer may offer you some form of these types of insurance products through your company group benefits plan. Realize, though, that most often those benefits are not portable—that is, if you move to a different employer, the benefits will not go with you. With people changing jobs more frequently these days and many people going into self-employment, the purchase of individual coverage is advisable. While it may be a bit more expensive, that insurance stays with you regardless of where you work. For self-employed people, it is even more critical as they have no employer plan to access. Remember, too, that the earlier you purchase such insurance; it is likely to be less expensive because of your younger age and fewer pre-existing conditions.

A recent study by LIMRA International (a worldwide association of insurance and financial services companies) reported that many Canadian families are not prepared for premature death. 30% of families with dependent children admit they will have immediate trouble meeting their everyday living expenses, and another 27% can cover expenses for only a few months if a primary wage earner dies.[1]

The same study indicated many Canadian couples are underinsured. The typical couple need to double their current coverage to meet the expert recommendation of having enough life insurance to replace income for seven to 10 years. With insurance you are using someone else's money to protect your assets and the cost can be significantly less than if you save the same amount of money yourself, as the following example shows.

---

[1] Source: Life Insurance Awareness Month, September 2007

Investment Needed to Match Insurance Payout

An insurance policy that will pay out $1,000,000 in 25 years carries an annual premium of $4,100.

How much do you need to invest each year in an outside investment (non-registered) to match the $1,000,000 policy?

If you earn 2.83% after taxes*, you need to invest $28,047 per year (end of year investment) or $23,947 more than the annual insurance premium of $4,100.

Rate of return	**5.00%**
Taxes at a 43.41% rate	**-2.17%**
After-tax rate	**2.83%**

Annual Amounts to Reach $1,000,000

$28,047

$4,100

Insurance Premium — Outside Investment

This chart is for illustrative purposes only and is not intended to project the performance of any particular investment.

Source: Ativa Concept Toolkit 9 (www.ativa.com)

In this example, a 35-year old male non-smoker purchases $1,000,000 of life insurance coverage. While a premium of $4,100 may seem high, the alternative is much worse! He will need to save $28,047 each year to reach the same $1,000,000 of the insurance policy. Protecting your family and your estate is essential for their future.

If Riki is single, buying life insurance may not be important. But if it is essential to her to leave a certain amount of money to her family or a favourite charity, she might wish to consider buying some life insurance to replace the amount of the income taxes her estate will need to pay. There are ways she can gift the life insurance policy as well which will accomplish her philanthropic goals, while receiving a tax benefit.

In fact, to protect and manage her wealth into the future, Riki might want to discuss tax savings strategies to be used to fund her insurance needs. For example, if she can maximize her RRSP, her tax savings might be used to fund her insurance premiums. Alternatively, she may wish to generate tax efficient income—like the capital gains on the disposition of some of her winning investments—to find the money for the insurance policies.

IMPORTANT PRINCIPLES IN PRODUCT SELECTION

A recent study[2] commissioned by Manulife Investments and conducted by two York University professors, Drs. Moshe Milevsky and Tom Salisbury, examined the "Retirement Risk Zone" and its impact on retirement income. The Retirement Risk Zone is the period leading into and just after retirement when the retirement nest egg is most vulnerable to market downturns.

There is no way of knowing what stage of the market cycle you will retire into or what the situation will be like when you need to take out money for an emergency and as a result, what sequence of returns you will receive on your investments. When poor performance occurs early in retirement, the decline is magnified because the money is also being withdrawn for income. This can make a big difference when it comes to how long your money will last and how well your income keeps up with inflation. Let's look at the following example.

The Difference Can Mean Years

This shows the impact of the sequence of returns. It assumes a $100,000 portfolio with an annual withdrawal of $9,000. Here are three scenarios:

Scenario 1, with a constant 7% annual return, the money will last until age 86.

Scenario 2, if the portfolio experiences the poor return early (-13%, followed by +7% and +27%), the money will last until age 81.

Scenario 3, if good returns are achieved at the beginning (+27%, followed by +7% and -13%), the money will last until age 95.

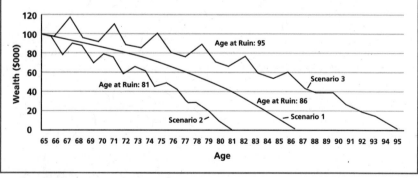

Courtesy of ⓒ Investments

---

[2]Source: Asset Allocation and the Transition to Income, Milevsky & Salisbury, September 2006

When you are accumulating financial wealth, the sequence of returns has no impact on your wealth but as you can see, this is quite a different story when you start drawing on that wealth. In the example above, your net worth could run out anywhere between age 81 to age 95.

While asset allocation plays an important role in the wealth accumulation phase of investing, the right mix of investment products for those drawing on their wealth is also needed in order to mitigate the risk of running out of money. Dr. Moshe Milevsky recommends that in such a scenario, the product allocation should consist of:

1. An immediate annuity (which is like a defined benefit pension plan in that in exchange for a sum of money you receive regular income payments).

2. A guaranteed minimum withdrawal product (which guarantees a certain amount of income for a specified period or in some cases, for life).

3. A systematic withdrawal plan (where income can be drawn from investments and the amount can change over time).

Since adequate after-tax income is needed to live your life, ensuring you have adequate cash flow is critical to the successful enjoyment of your retirement. However, while many financial assets can be turned into income, it may be difficult to do so quickly. You must bear this in mind when spontaneous opportunities for spending arise.

Assets, such as a house, can help give us shelter but don't necessarily put food on the table. Nor do they necessarily fund a quick trip to Vegas with your senior buddies. So a balance of each asset type is necessary to maintain your standard of living both before and in retirement.

In Riki's situation, the first thing she must look at in planning income is what the size of the after-tax income from her investments must be to live her desired lifestyle. If she knows what her expenses will be in retirement—both discretionary and non-discretionary—she will be in a good position to start looking at the structure of her investments to get the after-tax results she needs. To ensure those assets will be there when she wants them, she can now look at investment product alternatives that might provide her with the income she requires, as well as capital preservation and growth.

For example, it might not be the best time to purchase an annuity in the current market cycle, but if she feels one is needed, but she can put some money aside for purchasing this in the future. She may also want to put some of her investments into a money market fund or into bonds, to maintain their value—if she doesn't need much more growth on her investments. If she wants some growth but also some income protection, one of the new variable annuity products that guarantee an income for life might be an option. Now is the right time to explore the products that are being offered to determine what might fit into her income and wealth accumulation plan, their cost and their tax efficiency factors.

THE INHERITANCE WINDFALL

Boomers may soon receive a large wealth transfer from their parents, who were considerable savers. Before the recent market correction, it was estimated that a wealth transfer of almost $10 trillion dollars could occur in the U.S. over the next few decades. A comparable Canadian estimate would likely be in the range of $800 billion to $1 trillion.[3] Assuming markets will eventually recover, over the long-term, these estimates are still considered to be accurate.

This presents a second concern to future planners: how to best pass on wealth to children. Besides the obvious issues of how they will handle the money, is the concern about the taxes that will be levied on the estate if not properly planned for. Almost everyone seems to have heard of probate fees, which is a legal process through which a court confirms the authenticity of a will. These costs vary between provinces and I have heard about all sorts of manoeuvres to change ownership of assets in order to avoid probate fees. While avoiding or minimizing any sort of fees is certainly a wise thing to do, income taxes incurred by the estate can be far more costly than any probate fees and these taxes can often be avoided by some very inexpensive actions—such as naming your spouse or an eligible dependent as beneficiary for your RRSP.

---

[3]TD's Greying of Canada's Population Has Far Reaching Implications for Charities, Nov. 22, 2006

For instance, a single person holding $500,000 in an RRSP without an eligible beneficiary designated will result in probate fees in British Columbia of approximately $6,600 yet the income taxes that the estate must pay are about $201,000. That is because the entire RRSP in taken into income and taxed at the highest marginal tax rate when that person dies.

There are numerous estate planning strategies that can minimize the amount of taxes your estate will pay and some that will ensure a certain size estate be passed on to your heirs or charity of choice. Everyone has different plans for the legacy they wish to leave behind and it is important that you work with a legal and financial professional if you are concerned with how much you leave to Canada Revenue Agency instead of your chosen beneficiary.

In other situations, the transfer of wealth from one generation to the next will be used to pay down debt and contribute to retirement lifestyle. If Riki is planning on using some inheritance from her parents to fund her retirement, it may make sense for her to take out a life insurance policy on her parents for the estimated amount of income taxes that will become payable on their estate. Since she is still earning an income, she may choose to pay the premiums. This way her parents cash flow remains unchanged but Riki has secured some of her future assets which can be converted into income.

SELLING A BUSINESS

If you are like most business owners, your business is your largest asset; and the main source of income to fund your future income needs. A business cannot always be easily converted to cash like other assets. Often a business is sold to a third party for cash or shares or both. Sometimes however, there are no external buyers. Instead, you may have someone in the family to whom you can pass on the business (will that be cash or simply a transfer of assets?) or employees to whom you can sell it. In either case, remember that the new owner(s) will be managing your retirement fund, especially if you are receiving payment over time, so you must have a high degree of confidence in their abilities to manage your business.

If you have negotiated an outright sale of the business and have received the cash, remember to ensure that your sale proceeds are invested so as to minimize income taxes and maximize the cash available to you. After years of hard work, you are entitled to enjoy the results of the business you built from nothing. Structured properly, the sale of a qualifying small business corporation can result in significant tax free gains: every Canadian taxpayer qualifies for a lifetime capital gains deduction of $750,000, so a family of four adults can receive a tax free gain of $3 million dollars under these rules. Planning share and business structures is important.

If during the course of operating the business, you were able to generate taxable income that exceeds the small business deduction limit ($500,000 as of January 1, 2009) and more than needed for its operations, you may have already established a holding company to which excess cash was transferred. Structuring the holding company and the investments it holds are critical to the goal of minimizing income taxes and maximizing cash flow coming out of the holding company. It may also be a factor in whether the small business qualifies for the capital gains deduction.

The issue of owning a business and maximizing your access to its value is far too large a topic to be covered here. In fact, it is covered in *Master Your Investment in the Family Business*, another book in this series you may wish to pick up. Because business succession planning can be very complex, getting the assistance of a professional who works in this field is highly recommended.

IN SUMMARY

THINGS YOU NEED TO KNOW

- Ensuring you have sufficient cash flow (income) in times of low or no earnings is critical to the long term building of real wealth.
- The products available to address your needs are continually evolving and new ones are being introduced. Be sure to check about what is available when you are considering the use of one.
- Different products are priced differently. Be sure you understand the pricing structure for the products before you purchase.
- Some assets can be turned into income; some cannot.
- Self-employed individuals have some unique planning opportunities and challenges.

QUESTIONS YOU NEED TO ASK

- When and for what will I be using my savings?
- What financial products might be available to me and what are their costs?
- What insurance coverage do I have?
- Will I be receiving an inheritance?
- What taxes/fees will be collected from my estate?

THINGS YOU NEED TO DO

- Complete some long term cash flow planning to understand when you might be using your savings.
- Review your insurance policies to understand what you own and have your advisor complete an Insurance Needs analysis.
- Be sure to understand the pros and cons of various financial products and the cost/benefit of them.
- If you are self-employed, the earlier you start working with a professional financial/tax advisor, the better you will be able to maximize your income and net worth and minimize your taxes.

DECISIONS YOU NEED TO MAKE

- Decide where you need help and find someone who can offer that expertise to you.
- Determine what sort of lifestyle you want to have and what trade-offs must take place for that to happen.
- Learn more about the various financial products that are available to you.
- If you are self-employed, work to begin on your succession plan.

MASTER YOUR REAL WEALTH
Understanding the Process:
Income and Growth

TIPS

- Consider managing your exposure to market returns during the "Retirement Risk Zone".

- When drawing upon your financial assets for cash flow, the correct product allocation is as important as asset allocation. You may select a different financial product for your non-discretionary income needs than you would for your "lifestyle" needs.

- Protecting (insuring) your net worth as it grows is critical to your financial security.

- A business can be a substantial asset but care must be taken to maximize your ability to access its value.

TRAPS

- Don't make the mistake of abdicating your responsibility to managing your wealth to someone else. It's always important to at least understand the recommendations being made for a financial product or with financial advice.

- Avoiding basic estate planning can have a drastic impact on the inheritance you leave behind (or will receive).

- Not looking at insurance as an asset and income protector can damage your ability to grow your net worth.

Principle Mastery: Growing your real wealth also means protecting it in the event of an emergency or some other unfortunate event. When assets are sold or passed to a subsequent generation, tax-efficient strategies are critical to maximizing the value of the asset after the sale/transfer is complete.

CHAPTER 7

The Impact of Taxes

In financial planning, looking 'over the hood' is just as important as looking 'under the hood'. SOURCE UNKNOWN

> *Mikela and Fred are both professionals and 40 years old. Mikela works as a pharmacist, with taxable income of $155,000, while Fred is in pharmaceutical sales, earning $150,000 to $200,000 each year, depending on bonuses. They are each in a marginal tax bracket of over 43% which means Canada Revenue Agency will also enjoy a good income from their hard work.*

> *At some point, Fred may be able to incorporate and enjoy some tax advantages that incorporation can provide. But Mikela does not have that option unless she leaves her current employer. With an excellent benefit program provided by her employer, she is not thinking about any change at this point in time.*

> *Both have 'maxed' out their RRSPs and are now saving surplus funds in a non-registered account. Since there is no tax-sheltering for such an account, some tax planning is necessary to be able to maximize the value of these investments over time so that when they retire they have sufficient income to meet their lifestyle.*

THE ISSUES

Are there ways that Mikela and Fred can reduce the amount of taxes that they pay on their non-registered investments? They are already paying a high level of taxes on their incomes—this seems like they are paying it twice!

Paying taxes is part of life when you live in Canada. While no one would advocate tax evasion, which is a criminal offence, tax avoidance is legal. Tax evasion is a deliberate attempt to reduce taxes by making false statements about your income or deductions or by the destruction of records. Tax avoidance is simply exercising your right to minimize your taxes by way of proper tax planning.

Taxes are your largest lifetime expense. Therefore they must be carefully considered in any income and wealth management plan. Most people think about their taxes once a year during the tax filing deadline. But it's important to look at the effect of taxes on your income and capital over a lifetime. Consider the following, which illustrates this concept:

Lifetime Tax Burden – British Columbia

How much will you pay in income taxes over your working life?

If you earn $90,000 per year for 25 years with annual salary of increases of 2.00%, your gross, lifetime earnings over this period will be $2,882,727.

At an average tax rate of 25.22%*, you will pay $726,881 in income taxes over this same 25 year period.

The average tax rate is calculated by dividing the tax payable figure of $22,694 in the first year by taxable income of $90,000. The tax payable figure is increased each year by 2.00%, the same rate as the average annual salary increases.

Calculations use marginal tax rates as of March 2008. Rates take all federal and provincial taxes and surtaxes into account and the basic personal tax credits.

This chart is for illustrative purposes only and is not intended to calculate your actual tax liability.

Source: Ativa Concept Toolkit 9 (www.ativa.com)

Under this scenario, you will pay almost ¼ of your income to Canada Revenue Agency (CRA) over your lifetime. If you want to try to minimize the amount of taxes you will pay, some planning in advance is critical to your success in mastering your real wealth.

THE SOLUTIONS

There are a number of options to consider when you are looking at planning a more tax efficient approach to your investment activities:

- Understand the impact of tax on investment returns
- Choose tax efficient investments
- Structure tax efficient income
- Conduct your planning on a family basis

UNDERSTAND THE IMPACT OF TAX ON INVESTMENT RETURNS

There are a number of tax efficient investment opportunities available; however many taxpayers pass them by. For example, Canadians are generally well acquainted with the opportunity to invest in a Registered Retirement Savings Plan. One of the benefits of RRSP investing has always been the tax-deferred growth that such a tax-sheltered investment vehicle can provide, after you reap the benefits in tax savings from a reduced net and taxable income. Unfortunately many Canadians do not contribute their maximum possible contribution to their RRSPs, thereby leaving overpaid taxes and "clawed-back" tax credits or social benefits on the table.

Starting in 2009, Canadian adults can also invest in a Tax-Free Savings Account (TFSA), which allows a maximum contribution of $5000 (to be indexed to inflation in the future). That annual contribution limit, created by filing a tax return, accumulates investment earnings on a completely tax free basis. We'll tell you more about that in a moment. Suffice it to say for now that maximizing these two opportunities should be explored with your tax and financial advisors, as they are the cornerstones of tax efficient investing today.

Once you have contributed the maximum to your RRSP, and invested in a TFSA for every adult in the family, there are numerous other investment options available, but taking advantage of them depends greatly on factors such as your immediate savings requirements (retirement, education or home purchase for example), work structure (e.g. self-employed versus an employee), whether or not you need life insurance (for the tax-free growth of investment income in a universal life policy) or if you are comfortable with investing solely in equities that generate only capital gains (vs. dividends or other income). You need to keep an eye on the tax efficiency of the income generated, but also on the tax consequences of the asset's disposition later in life or upon death.

When it comes to investment income, most people know, for example, that dividend income and capital gains are taxed more favourably than interest income, but did you also know that the size and availability of certain government benefits (e.g. OAS pensions) can be negatively affected by an overweighting of income from dividends? That's because dividends are "grossed up" for tax purposes, which increases your net income—the figure upon which social benefits like the OAS and refundable and non-refundable tax credits is based. (Later on in the tax return, the taxes computed on those grossed-up dividends are offset by a dividend tax credit; thereby integrating the personal and corporate tax system, and giving dividends preferential tax treatment.)

Managing the type of income you receive, therefore, is critical to both the tax impact and for the purposes of receiving other benefits such as government sponsored programs.

Let's look at some investment results for Mikela and Fred. Let's assume they will each contribute $25,000 to a taxable investment account and each will contribute $10,000 annually to age 60.

Under this scenario the pre-tax compounding results in $1.085 million at age 60 on a total combined investment of $450,000. This compares to an investment where taxable distributions would reduce the annual after-tax return to 5.25% ($861,000). (Income used in the calculations is the average of all mutual funds 1996-2006.)

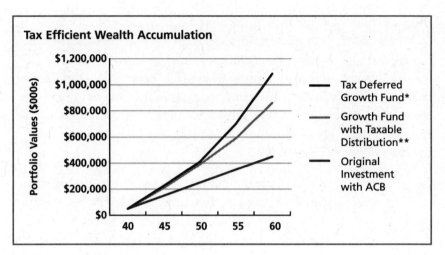

Tax Efficient Wealth Accumulation

Portfolio Values ($000s)

- Tax Deferred Growth Fund*
- Growth Fund with Taxable Distribution**
- Original Investment with ACB

Source: NexGen Financial
*Assumes no taxable distributions need to be paid
**Assumes Industry Average Annual Loss to Taxes of 25% of Pre Tax Return

It certainly pays for Fred and Mikela to look at the impact of taxes on their non-registered funds!

CHOOSE TAX EFFICIENT INVESTMENTS

There are now many more investments designed to try to reduce the taxable impact of investment growth. Many of these are in the various structures that mutual funds can be purchased in.

A fund that offers a portion of its distributions as a Return of Capital, for example, provides a non-taxable payment. In other words, because your own tax-paid capital that is being paid back to you, no taxable income is created.

Investors are often concerned that this will result in an erosion of their capital base; however, most funds have been structured so that the payout is less than the capital growth being produced by the fund. (If there is no capital growth for a sustained period of time, the regularly scheduled payout will be reduced.)

Under this option for income generation, the consequences are deferred until the investment is sold, at which time a capital gain or loss is triggered.

This is because the cost base of the asset has been reduced each time you withdrew capital. Fortunately capital gains of the year are offset by capital losses; then only 50% of the net gain is included in taxable income, and even this may be offset by available net capital losses of prior years. So not only have you deferred your tax on the growth in the value of the asset, but you will most likely have reduced it as well, all the while enjoying a larger after-tax income than with a traditional investment such as a bond or dividend fund.

Corporate or capital class mutual funds can also be used to create income with the deferral of taxes. These assets are different from typical mutual fund trusts which are structured as a single fund unit. When an investor purchases one of the capital class funds, they are essentially buying into a group of funds rather than a single mutual fund. Since all of the capital class funds are part of the same corporate structure, investors are able to switch from one capital class fund to another without triggering a taxable disposition.

It's also important to know that segregated funds (which is an investment fund held within an insurance contract) are taxed somewhat differently than mutual funds. Segregated funds 'allocate' income such as capital gains and capital losses to investors while mutual funds 'distribute' income. The distinction is subtle until you actually receive a tax slip from the financial institution that offers the segregated fund. For example, segregated funds can flow through capital losses to the investor which allows the investor to offset the capital loss against capital gains from the last three years or carried forward to future years. With a mutual fund, capital losses are offset against capital gains within the fund and only the net capital gains will be shown on the investor's T3.

Be sure to discuss the difference at the time of purchase so that you will understand the various tax slips you may be receiving.

Individual securities, on the other hand, all have different taxation structures. Most common shares generate capital gains upon disposition, if their value has risen over the original cost. Since only half of a net capital gain (that is, capital gains offset by capital losses) is included in income, common shares may have a lower tax impact than some other investments.

Preferred shares often issue dividends, which are the after-tax profits of a corporation to its shareholders. These receive preferential tax treatment and in some provinces have a very low marginal tax rate. (Dividends in B.C. for example had a marginal tax rate of only 4.4% in 2008). You need to be careful, though, that the gross-up that is associated with these does not create an income at line 236 on your tax return that will negate or reduce any government benefits you might be entitled to.

Interest income, which is received from such investments as Guaranteed Investment Certificates (GICs), bonds, Canada Savings Bonds, etc., is fully included in income on your tax return and therefore attracts the highest marginal tax rates. Worse, investments which pay compounded interest income are considered particularly inefficient for tax purposes because of the requirement to report that interest annually, even though you haven't received it. It is therefore often best to have such investments held within a tax sheltered plan such as an RRSP, RESP or Tax-Free Savings Account, particularly if you believe interest rates may rise again in the future.

As mentioned earlier, as of January 1, 2009, the Tax-Free Savings Account (TFSA) are available to all individuals 18 and over (or legal age of majority for each province). This vehicle represents one of the most important tax savings opportunities that Canadians have seen in some time. While the initial amount that can be contributed may seem small ($5,000), the longer term impact of using such an investment vehicle cannot be discounted. Where else does CRA allow you to earn income and NEVER have it taxed?

Other features of this account include:

- Unused TFSA contribution room can be carried forward to future years. So if you don't have the money now but are expecting some next year, you can deposit $10,000 next year. Simply file a tax return to generate this contribution room.
- In some cases, these investments can be purchased on a monthly basis—as is the case with mutual funds. Even though it is called a savings plan, the types of investments that can be used are much the same as you can hold in your RRSP.

- Any amount withdrawn can be put back into the TFSA at a later date without reducing contribution room—not the case for RRSPs.
- Neither income earned in a TFSA nor withdrawals will affect eligibility for federal income tested benefits and tax credits.

Mikela and Fred should ensure they take advantage of the new TFSA. They may also wish to invest money in corporate class mutual funds so that any changes they make in their portfolio do not create a taxable situation. These funds often do not pay any distribution so there is a further tax efficiency with this vehicle.

There are also some funds that allow you to choose how your income is paid out—for instance, if Mikela or Fred have some previous taxable capital losses, they can choose to have the fund pay out capital gains (instead of interest) which can be offset against those previous losses.

As you can see, the many tax efficient options available for creating tax preferred income and capital can be used to enhance your investment returns and average them over time. Tax efficiency plays a significant role in determining the size of your real wealth.

STRUCTURE TAX EFFICIENT INCOME

When you are reviewing a product recommendation from your financial professional, if it is being invested in a tax-sheltered account such as an RRSP or TFSA, your focus usually does not need to be on the tax impact of that investment. In the case of the RRSP, for example, any withdrawals will be considered 'ordinary income' regardless of the type of income generated by the investment within it. There are two exceptions to this rule: when money is withdrawn from the RRSP under the Lifelong Learning Plan or Home Buyer's Plan. However those tax free withdrawals may be reported in income in the future if minimum repayment requirements are not met.

For the TFSA, there is no tax on any growth within the account, not even when it is withdrawn, so it is completely tax efficient. However, the original investment is made on a tax-paid basis—that is, there is no tax deduction for making the contribution.

For all other types of investments, besides looking at the merits of the investment product itself, you want to understand:

- the type of income that will be generated
- what the marginal tax rate on that source of income is
- how frequently that income is paid out
- whether the investment is available in a more tax-favourable format
- what sort of bookkeeping will be required to ensure proper reporting to CRA

It is most often possible to reduce the impact of tax of your investments but, your choices do depend on your risk profile and how comfortable you are with alternate investment strategies which offer tax efficiencies. These are often no riskier than the standard type of investments; the trade-off may be that more tax efficient investments will not offer the same 'guarantees' that products such as GICs provide. You need to understand your options and make decisions that are appropriate for your own situation.

And, as discussed earlier, be sure to understand how each source of income you earn is taxed, including your salary, to determine if there is a way to reduce the taxable impact on that revenue stream, perhaps with proper timing.

CONDUCT YOUR PLANNING ON A FAMILY BASIS

Family members can participate in the creation of real wealth by taking advantage of tax free zones (as of 2009, the federal Basic Personal Amount is over $10,000 per individual), and tax preferred investment opportunities, like making deposits into an RRSP and a TFSA.

Income splitting between family members and specifically spouses can be accomplished in a variety of ways. For example, the use of a spousal RRSP has always been available to split incomes for couples in retirement. The contributing spouse, most often the one with the higher income, will get the tax break from making the contribution for the lower income spouse. That spouse, when drawing out the money, will most likely be in a lower tax bracket and will therefore pay less in income taxes than if the entire amount had been drawn by one spouse. That income splitting opportunity benefits the household as a whole, and often can preserve the level of other income sources, like Old Age Security.

The 2006 federal budget introduced some additional pension income splitting rules for individuals 65 years of age or older. These rules allow senior couples to pool their eligible retirement income from private pension accumulations, with each individual reporting up to $1/2$ of the eligible income on their tax return. Eligibility depends on the source of the pension and age of the recipient, so it's important to establish what can be included by speaking with your financial advisor.

Another income splitting method involves paying one's spouse or children to work in the family business, or in some cases, assist in the earning of employment income. That can transfer income away from the higher income spouse to family members who earn less—something that can end up lowering the overall tax bill for the family unit.

Capital can also be transferred to family members in some cases. For example, if you would like to help your adult child out with the purchase of a house, gifting the money while you are alive is a tax efficient way to transfer some of your wealth without triggering any taxes. You must be aware, though, that if your adult child is married, the home often becomes a marital asset and is divided should the relationship terminate. You may not want that money to remain in the hands of your son or daughter's ex-spouse. It is a good idea to obtain legal advice in advance. What is good for avoiding of the taxman may not be good when it comes to family law issues.

Any transfers of wealth, either directly or indirectly through a loan may be subject to Attribution Rules, which require the reporting of certain income sources generated by the transfer on the return of the transferee (the higher earner). See *Master Your Taxes* for more information and speak to your professional advisors to make sure your tax efficient planning is not undone by the taxman!

IN SUMMARY

THINGS YOU NEED TO KNOW

- Taxes are your largest lifetime expense, and will erode your capital on death also if you fail to structure your investments properly.
- You have many options for tax efficient investments.
- Understand your marginal tax rate on each investment income source.
- Some investments—like the RRSP—can provide immediate tax savings; others like the TFSA will earn income that is completely tax free. Make sure you understand which type of investments you have in your portfolio.
- Tax efficient investing and other opportunities for tax deferral and family income splitting will help you tap into more wealth when you need it.
- Remember, it's what you keep, not what you earn, that counts in every investment strategy.

QUESTIONS YOU NEED TO ASK

- In what order should I make my investment choices? RRSP first? TFSA next?
- What is the difference between a registered and non-registered account on initial deposit and when income is earned?
- In what order should I withdraw funds from my investments for maximum tax efficiency?

THINGS YOU NEED TO DO

- Save money—set purposeful goals to fund tax preferred investments.
- Make more money—find out how you can increase your earnings to invest more.
- Tap into other people's money—should you borrow to invest? Will interest be deductible? Who should you borrow from—parents, employers, financial institutions?
- Free up money—stop overpaying taxes at source. Ask your employer whether you can reduce the size of your tax refund by remitting only the correct amount of tax. Then pay off credit cards and save more.

DECISIONS YOU NEED TO MAKE

- Invest tax efficiently—at least in an RRSP and TFSA if you are able to do so.
- Understand how to withdraw earnings tax efficiently.
- Work with an investment advisor to ensure tax efficient outcomes.

MASTER YOUR REAL WEALTH
The Impact of Taxes

TIPS

- Know your marginal tax bracket and the impact different types of income will have on the amount of income taxes you will pay.
- Discuss with your financial professional if the product being recommended is tax efficient and how it will apply to your tax bracket.
- Open up a TFSA.
- Consider if a spousal RRSP is appropriate.
- If you are over 65, be sure to take advantage of the pension income splitting rules.
- Consider your tax planning on a family basis.

TRAPS

- Don't make the mistake of ignoring the TFSA because the initial contribution limit is only $5,000.
- There are alternate forms of investments that can reduce your income taxes without assuming a great deal more of risk. Don't be afraid to explore them.
- If you have a family business, don't pay your family members an income unless they do perform a task in your company.
- Don't avoid keeping records for investments; you will need the information to correctly complete your income tax return.
- Don't gift money to an adult child if he or she is in an unstable relationship. Should the relationship break up, it could be split between the child and his/her ex partner.

CHAPTER 8

The Impact of Inflation

I have enough money to last me the rest of my life, unless I buy something.
JACKIE MASON

Jennifer and Mark are happily anticipating retirement. Mark, a computer and math fanatic, has completed a spreadsheet which shows that based on their current and proposed savings, they will have enough money to live the retirement that they are planning until each has reached age 90.

Mark spoke to his banker and was told to use an investment growth rate of 6% since they are not high risk takers. As well, he was advised to plan to at least age 90 and that as a rule of thumb, using 70—80% of current income for retirement purposes should be adequate. They have no mortgage or other debt so Mark feels quite confident in using the 70% figure. Mark was excited to discuss their new retirement budget and plans for life after work. Jennifer was not so sure, given recent economic turmoil...

THE ISSUES

While it's to be expected that some expenses will change over the retirement period, are Mark's projections adequate—and realistic for the long term? The following are the projections he presented to Jennifer.

What it Costs to Live (Current Expenses)

Housing	26.40%	$19,800
Taxes	21.20%	$15,900
Food	13.40%	$10,050
Transportation	13.20%	$9,900
Recreation	8.00%	$6,000
Insurance/Pensions	5.30%	$3,975
Clothing	4.20%	$3,150
Health Care	4.10%	$3,075
Gifts/Charities	2.20%	$1,650
Miscellaneous	2.00%	$1,500
Totals	**100%**	**$75,000**

Based on needing only 70% of current income in retirement, Mark is confident they will have enough money to last them to age 90. Their pensions, CPP, RRSPs and OAS will provide income of $60,000 each year.

$75,000 x 70% = $52,500

Inflation was the bogeyman that we all got to know in the late '70s and '80s. With price increases in the double digits, anyone on a fixed income immediately experienced a cash flow shortfall. For instance, inflation increased by 11% in 1974. As a result, an item costing $10 in 1973 suddenly cost $11.10. But if your income had not also increased by the same amount, you suddenly could no longer afford to purchase that item.

While inflation continued, albeit at lower annual rates throughout the 90's, inflation had another negative impact for Canadian taxpayers—bracket creep. That is, personal credits and tax brackets were not indexed to inflation, which resulted in a hidden tax on inflation that few taxpayers took into account. Inflation is a real force to be considered in mastering your real wealth—what's left when you need it.

While the Bank of Canada has had very good control of our inflation, the current economic stimulus provided by governments worldwide to prevent a financial meltdown will have inflationary pressures down the road. As the government prints more money to accommodate the crisis, the money supply increases faster than the growth in productivity, bringing with it an associated increase in inflation. This has an important impact as we try to determine financial needs far into the future.

Consider this: even with inflation of 2%, the cost of a loaf of bread doubles every 36 years. (At 6% inflation, it doubles every 12 years.) Since retirements are now expected to last as long as 30 years or more, the inflation rate is a very important factor to consider.

Now let's look at Mark's projections when 2% inflation is included.

What it Costs to Live (Current Expenses)			(Projected Expenses in 10 Years)
Housing	26.40%	$19,800	$24,136
Taxes	21.20%	$15,900	$19,382
Food	13.40%	$10,050	$12,251
Transportation	13.20%	$9,900	$12,068
Recreation	8.00%	$6,000	$7,314
Insurance/Pensions	5.30%	$3,975	$4,846
Clothing	4.20%	$3,150	$3,840
Health Care	4.10%	$3,075	$3,748
Gifts/Charities	2.20%	$1,650	$2,011
Miscellaneous	2.00%	$1,500	$1,828
Totals	100%	$75,000	$91,425

$91,425 x 70% = $63,997

Now, it is very possible that some of the items being paid for while working (pension plan contributions for example) will not be an expense in retirement. That is why using a rule of thumb of 70% of income may be appropriate. But in this case, when Jennifer and Mark retire in 10 years, 70% of the expected expenses are still more than the $60,000 Mark calculated their incomes to be in retirement. And this difference will increase each year with inflation.

The good thing is that Canada Pension Plan (CPP) and Old Age Security (OAS) are indexed to inflation so as inflation increases, so does the income from those programs. But neither Mark nor Jennifer has a pension plan that is indexed and this is where the problem lies. In some way they will need to account for the difference between their incomes and expenses—either by reducing their costs or purchasing a financial product that can help them with this problem.

THE SOLUTIONS

Not taking inflation into account is one of the most common mistakes I see when reviewing client-prepared projections for future income. Inflation can cause a serious cash flow shortfall at a time when there is little ability to change the outcome.

There are four main investment product solutions that can help counter-act the effects of inflation:

- Indexed annuity
- Variable annuity
- Asset allocation in retirement
- Asking questions of your financial professional

HOW AN INDEXED ANNUITY CAN HELP

If you are in a position where your financial assets will not adequately fund your estimated retirement expenses, a good starting point is to look at your non-discretionary expenses. These are items you "need" and include such things as food, shelter, medical expenses and other such costs. You must ensure you have sufficient income to cover at least those items on an inflation-adjusted basis.

One way to do that is to purchase an indexed annuity. Annuities of all sorts are usually purchased through a life insurance company and involve giving a lump sum of money to the financial institution in return for which it will provide periodic income (monthly or otherwise) on an inflation-adjusted basis. There are many different types of annuities available so it is important that you speak with someone who is knowl-edgeable about these products. My personal philosophy is to forego the bells and whistles that come with such products and just buy the basic product that you need. Of course, there can be exceptions but just realize that all the extras cost money—so don't buy them unless there is a feature that will prove beneficial to you down the road.

The price of annuities and what they will pay you is also based on current interest rates. With interest rates at an all time low right now, you may wish to defer purchasing such a product at this time. But you can certainly get a quote to determine how much that may cost you and then you can put the money aside in a savings account, GIC or money market fund to use later, when interest rates are higher or when you can no longer defer completing the purchase.

HOW A VARIABLE ANNUITY CAN HELP

Variable annuities have recently been introduced to the Canadian marketplace and are gaining wide acceptance by consumers partly because of the "guaranteed income for life" feature. These can be very complicated products and there are costs associated with that guarantee, but if you do not have a pension plan, it may be worthwhile discussing with your financial professional if this is a product suitable for you to include in your retirement product shelf.

With many of the improved features that have been added since they were first introduced, these products have become more appealing for individuals in mid-life. The products often include a bonus each year when no money is drawn out and if you are still saving for retirement with no plans to take money out of your RRSP, the bonusing can add to the value of the investment and how it affects the lifetime income guarantee. It's worth looking into.

HOW ASSET ALLOCATION CAN HELP

As discussed earlier, asset allocation is the mix of investment products you hold in your portfolio. The basic types are equities (stocks, some mutual funds), income (bonds, preferred shares, some mutual funds) and cash or cash equivalents (GICs, money market funds). It is understood that the closer you are to retirement, the less risk you are usually willing to take. Therefore many people believe that when they retire they will switch all of their investments into cash/cash equivalent/income-type products. But when you are funding a retirement of 30 + years, these types of investments will not keep pace with inflation. The solution is to keep some of your portfolio in equities to ensure growth of the portfolio will be maintained. It is only equities that have the ability to provide protection against inflation.

In fact, in a recent study it was found that 60% of the growth of your portfolio occurs during your retirement.[1] This is not to say that all of your retirement funds need to be in equities. How much is held for growth depends on your situation—how much of your income is currently guaranteed, your risk tolerance level, the outlook for inflation and other factors. There have been many instances where my retiree clients put 2 years worth of income draws into a money market fund and have left the rest invested. That way, they are assured the income they will require will be there and should the markets drop, there is a two year window in which the recovery can take place. It's a combination that has worked well.

WHAT TO DISCUSS WITH YOUR FINANCIAL PROFESSIONAL

Your financial professional will be able to provide projections to help you gauge your financial situation in retirement and to determine any shortfalls. The earlier you do this, the more time you have to make any needed adjustments. You need to understand what measure of inflation he or she has used in the projections and have him or her explain the rationale for that choice.

You will want to find out about the various products that might be suitable for you and the cost of those products. If there a feature you don't need and it can be separated out, elect that option and reduce your costs. In my opinion, many of the new variable annuity products can be parceled together by a financial professional—but the 'parcel' must continue to be adjusted over time. Unless you are certain your advisor will be with you for many years to come and has the expertise to put together such a product, the cost for the variable annuity can quickly be worth it, if it is a suitable product for you.

---

[1] Source: Collie, Bob and Matt Smith. "The 10/30/60 Rule: Where Do Defined Contribution (DC) Plan Benefits Come From? It's Not Where You Think." *Russell DC Insights*, January 2008

The good thing about all the boomers reaching retirement is the many new retirement-focused products being introduced to the Canadian marketplace. There will most likely be some very innovative products developed to address such concerns as longevity and inflation—just be sure to understand them before making a purchase. The most important starting point is to look at your retirement projections on an inflation-adjusted basis so you know what safeguards you need to build into your plans.

IN SUMMARY

THINGS YOU NEED TO KNOW

- When income fails to increase at the same rate as inflation, you will have a shortfall in your purchasing power.
- The current financial crisis will have an impact on the rate of inflation in the future.
- Public pensions are currently indexed to inflation; many private pensions are not.
- Inflation-proof investments can help.

QUESTIONS YOU NEED TO ASK

- How does inflation affect my projections for future income?
- How will inflation affect my taxes?
- What can I do to hedge my portfolio against the threat of inflation?
- How can I be sure of my real wealth—what's left when I need it?

THINGS YOU NEED TO DO

- Find out how indexed annuities can be used to cover future non-discretionary expenditures.
- Discuss variable annuities with your advisors, especially their bonus features.
- Consider how changes in your asset allocation might assist with your inflation protection activities.

DECISIONS YOU NEED TO MAKE

- Speak to a financial advisor about product alternatives that specifically consider inflation–protection.
- Understand how the impact of inflation and taxes together can erode your wealth.

MASTER YOUR REAL WEALTH
The Impact of Inflation

TIPS

- Prepare or have prepared for you some inflation-adjusted projections for your retirement.
- Review the various products that are available in the marketplace to determine their features and the related costs.
- Determine if some of your retirement investment portfolio should continue to be invested for growth.
- Have a discussion with your financial professional about what products he or she would recommend and why.

TRAPS

- Don't be intimidated by the complexity of some of the products. Your financial professional should able to explain the product to you—or think twice about purchasing it from that individual. Everyone is on a learning curve with a new product; the difference is whether or not the person you are working with makes an attempt to get the correct answers for you.
- If completing projections is not your forte, paying a professional for this service is one of the best expenditures you can make. Don't let your inexperience get in the way of obtaining this critical information.
- Don't by shy to speak with your financial professional about the asset allocation of your investment portfolio. Perhaps some tweaking is in order.

Principle Mastery: Sixty percent of the growth of your portfolio occurs in retirement—saving more now will ensure a brighter future in retirement. Taking the impact of both taxes and inflation into account in the wealth accumulation and growth phases of your investment activities will help you preserve and transition more wealth.

CHAPTER 9

The Impact of Currency Fluctuation

I am having an out-of-money experience. UNKNOWN WISE PERSON

> *Virginia is an Australian citizen but her husband, David, is Canadian. They live and work in Canada but vacation in Australia for six to eight weeks of the year. Virginia is very familiar with Australian companies and wishes to invest in those she feels will do very well.*
>
> *David is concerned with the exchange rate between the Canadian and Australian dollar. If the Canadian dollar were to increase in value in relation to the Australian dollar, the return on those Australian investments will be diminished even if the stocks do well.*
>
> *Virginia is adamant that global investing is important because the Canadian marketplace is small and not well diversified. She feels that investing some money outside of Canada more than compensates for any risk associated with any change in the currency.*

THE ISSUES

Is it possible that Virginia is correct and that global diversification is more important than looking at the currency risk?

Global investing allows you to diversify across economies and markets to tap into areas of growth not available in Canada. A globally diversified portfolio can also cushion the impact of losses in any one market or currency, since foreign economies, markets and currencies can and do move in different cycles. History has also shown that global investing increases your potential for higher returns.

Thirty years ago currency management was little more than the introduction of a free-floating exchange rate. Now currency management has become an integral tool of many portfolio managers.

Managing currency risk, or hedging, is a process used to mitigate the risks stemming from an undesirable exposure to a foreign currency. Another way of looking at it is to think of hedging as insurance. It is more about mitigating the risk than about generating returns since currency management may mean giving up some of the upside in order to mitigate the downside. There are many tools available to accomplish this including spot contracts, forward contracts, foreign currency swaps and options.

If we look at the following table, we can see the results on an unhedged portfolio at a time when the local currency rises in relation to the foreign one. Any amount of hedging would have resulted in improved returns for the local investor. Of course, the reverse is also true when the local currency falls in relation to the foreign currency.

	Unhedged	Fully Hedged	50% Hedged
Average return (PA) %	2.3	3.2	2.9

Hypothetical Example of Currency Hedging

THE SOLUTIONS

Even if you never hedge for your own portfolio you should understand how it works because many big companies and investment funds will hedge from time to time. There are two main issues to consider:

- When to hedge
- What to ask your financial professional

UNDERSTAND WHEN TO HEDGE

As an example let's look at Virginia's desire to take exposure in an Australian company but not to the risk related to unexpected movements in the currency. She might decide to hedge her risk by selling the Australian dollar forward, in order to fix today tomorrow's price of the Australian dollar and eliminate the currency risk.

There is a risk in using this approach, however, and that is, because the forward contract is locked-in, if the exchange rate suddenly turns really favourable there is nothing the investor can do. The contract is also for a fixed amount and because you are buying into the future, it may be difficult to obtain a rate that you consider competitive. This is the cost of using a hedging technique and any benefits must be weighed against the cost.

Evidence also suggests that foreign exchange risk is really only a serious issue for short-term investors. In the longer term, currency fluctuations tend to smooth out, so that the share price will reflect a company's true worth.

Ultimately we are all affected by currency fluctuations, even if we only invest at home, since Canadian companies must purchase and sell on international markets.

For Virginia and David, perhaps the most important consideration is the fact that Virginia is only looking at buying in one country. She is not truly diversifying her portfolio and depending on her outlook for the Australian currency and the length of time she plans to hold the Australian stocks, she may decide that hedging is not worth the expense.

As well, If Virginia and David instead decide to diversify across other markets in addition to Australia, the diversification strategy may suggest no hedging is needed.

UNDERSTAND WHAT TO ASK YOUR FINANCIAL PROFESSIONAL

When a financial product is being recommended to you, ask if it is a Canadian or foreign investment. In the case of the latter, a discussion of the currency exposure is relevant—even if you decide not to do anything about it. As well, if you are purchasing a foreign mutual fund, asking if it is available as a hedged fund and if it is advisable to purchase on that basis is a worthwhile discussion. Realizing that hedging can work against you if the exchange rate turns favourable is also an important fact to remember. Sometimes acquiring global content will give you currency diversification which removes the need for expensive hedging products.

As we just saw, investors have a range of options to mitigate the risk of currency movement. But they are complex strategies requiring considerable expertise and are often best left to the experts. This is one reason why purchasing a mutual fund for your foreign exposure may be the ideal solution. Some of these funds can be purchased on a hedged or unhedged basis and you know there will be expertise at the fund company level to exercise those contracts.

IN SUMMARY

THINGS YOU NEED TO KNOW

- History has shown that global investing increases your potential for higher returns.
- Managing currency risk, or hedging, is a process used to mitigate the risks stemming from an undesirable exposure to a foreign currency.
- There are many tools available to accomplish this.

QUESTIONS YOU NEED TO ASK

- Should my portfolio contain an element of exposure to foreign markets?
- How can I adequately protect myself against wealth erosion when currencies fluctuate?
- What is the cost of not being invested globally?

THINGS YOU NEED TO DO

- Find out more about spot contracts, forward contracts, foreign currency swaps and options.

DECISIONS YOU NEED TO MAKE

- Work with an advisor who can incorporate the impact of currency fluctuations in your Real Wealth Management™ plan.

MASTER YOUR REAL WEALTH
The Impact of Currency Fluctuation

TIPS

- Understand the risk of purchasing a foreign investment and decide whether or not the currency risk needs to be managed.
- The time frame you anticipate holding your foreign investment will also factor into whether or not to hedge.
- If hedging is too complex for you, let the professional money managers do the work by purchasing a global or international mutual fund.

TRAPS

- Don't be deterred by the complexity of the products for hedging. A discussion as to whether or not hedging would be prudent may be all that is needed.
- At the same time, if a hedging product is being recommended, discuss the cost of the product and the potential for rapid currency fluctuation.
- Recognize that using a forward contract to hedge means it is a locked in contract and if exchange rates turn favourable there is nothing you can do.

Principle Mastery: When a financial product is being recommended to you, it's important to understand if it is a Canadian or foreign investment. A discussion of the currency exposure is relevant—even if you decide not to do anything about it—when you invest abroad. It can help you master your real wealth.

CHAPTER 10

The Impact of Investment Cost

Misers aren't fun to live with, but they make wonderful ancestors.
DAVID BRENNER

Robert and Mavis each have $50,000 to invest. Robert considers himself to be an educated investor who feels comfortable investing on his own. Mavis, on the other hand, recognizes what she knows but has decided she has no time to be an active portfolio manager and has elected to purchase some mutual funds. They each must pay for the investments they make. They decided to compare notes on who invested most cost-effectively.

In Mavis's case, the Management Expense Ratios (MERs) of her mutual funds are as follows:

Type of Fund	% of Portfolio	MER
Canadian Growth Fund	60%	1.60
International Equity Fund	15%	2.10
Canadian Bond Fund	25%	1.50
Total Weighted MER		1.65

Consequently, the cost to Mavis for her portfolio is $825 for the first year. Robert, though, is an active investor and rarely holds on to an investment for more than two to three months[1]. Over the course of the year he anticipates buying and selling about 10-15 stocks. Using an online broker, he is charged $19 for each trade he executes. So if he places 10 buys and sells, it will cost him $380; at 15, the buys and sells will cost $570. So, on a dollar for dollar basis, it would seem to cost Robert $255 less even if he places 15 buy and 15 sell orders each year.

That makes a compelling argument for doing it yourself, from a cost point of view...or does it?

THE ISSUES

Is it really that simple to determine the difference of the costs of investing between two people?

Research says no. In a study by Terrance Odean (see note 1), Robert's return on his investments is most likely 2.65% less than it would have been if he had not traded as frequently. So he may not be farther ahead, when you consider both his cost of trading and his return on investment. Mavis, who has paid a professional money manager to manage her portfolio likely netted more when both return and cost is calculated. This is the process that must be considered in making the decision to invest yourself or with professional help.

Many investors are unaware of the fees they pay for their investment products, often because they are hidden. It may be that no money is paid up front by the investor and that instead, the cost of the product is deducted from the return of the investment. Furthermore, the average investor may find it hard to decipher information about fees in the prospectus and other financial reports. Since there is no such thing as a free lunch, some knowledge of your investment costs is necessary.

---

[1]Studies have shown that men trade more often than women. Research by Terrance Odean, a behavioral economist at the University of California of Berkeley, found that men trade 45% more than women and that trading reduces men's net returns by 2.65 percentage points a year as opposed to 1.72 percentage points for women.

For example, and contrary to popular belief, there is often a fee charged to you when you purchase a bond through a broker. Since most bonds do not trade on organized exchanges, they are traded between financial institutions at a wholesale price and then sold to the retail consumer at a markup, which reduces your yield. The difference between the wholesale and retail prices is the firm's profit.

Mutual funds, as discussed in Chapter 3, are sold in a variety of ways and also are subject to a Management Expense Ratio (MER). This MER is deducted directly from the assets and is already included in the fund's rate of return. Consequently, you do not pay for this directly out of your pocket.

For non-registered accounts, there is often an option for the investor to deduct a portion of the MER paid to the advisor, generally 1%, directly against the income from the investment. This is tax efficient, as that portion of the fees can be deducted on the personal tax return. So, in Mavis's case, if she has negotiated to have that portion of the fee deducted against the income earned, she will be able to write off $500 of the MER.

Stocks are purchased or sold either via a discount brokerage firm or full-service firm. The costs can vary significantly, depending on the size of the portfolio, size of the trade and amount of service being provided. This range can be quite wide, from $9.95/trade to $39/trade and up.

Principal protected notes, which normally guarantee the principal if held to maturity, have fees that include commissions paid to the advisor (commonly 4%), ongoing management fees (often 2%) and performance fees to the portfolio managers (these can range between 18-20%).

Hedge funds and derivative products can be very expensive to purchase and fees are often hard to ascertain. Because of the complexity of these products, performance fees, particularly for hedge funds, form a good component of the professional money manager's compensation.

So the issue is this: how do the various fees you pay on your investments, whether you do it yourself or use professional money management, affect your ability to accumulate real wealth?

THE SOLUTIONS

The amount of money you pay to invest will have an effect on your real wealth accumulations. You should extrapolate your average annual costs for buying the investments, including interest and carrying charges, and project them into the future to understand the cost erosion. You can make choices to reduce that cost as part of your wealth management process.

There are a few things you can do to determine if the cost of your investment product is too high or not.

- Determine what type of investor you are.
- What to discuss with your financial professional.
- Shop around: get more information.

DETERMINE WHAT TYPE OF INVESTOR YOU ARE

The first thing to determine in establishing an investment cost budget, is what type of investor are you? If you are not very knowledgeable in this area and/or have little time to manage the portfolio, the fee of a professional money manager is well worth the cost. But you cannot completely abdicate your responsibility for your portfolio to someone else. Updates on a periodic basis, the timing of which can vary from investor to investor, should be scheduled and while you don't need to be able to explain the discussion in detail to someone else, you should feel that you at least understand what was said and that you are comfortable with the information provided. Determine if there are any more cost-effective ways to accomplish the same results.

If you prefer a hands-on approach and have sufficient knowledge and time to do so, consider whether or not you need some additional professional advice regarding your long term strategy for investing, or if you can get your information from other *trustworthy* sources. That will help you to decide between a full-service or discount firm.

Never discount the value of advice. There have been numerous studies undertaken which have demonstrated that investors who work with a financial professional do better than do-it-yourselfers. Partly that is because of the discipline encouraged by the professional but also because of the information they are able to access as a result of their professional contacts. A team approach is usually a better way to leverage the possibilities for getting better long term results. It is also a good way to connect your investment activities with your tax consequences. Professional advisors who work together on a common plan with you, taking your personal net worth into account in planning, can help you create real wealth, after tax, after inflation and after costs.

WHAT TO DISCUSS WITH YOUR FINANCIAL PROFESSIONAL

As there is always a cost associated with a product or service, don't hesitate to ask your advisor to break down how he or she is compensated for the sale of a product or the delivery of the services to you.

Let's focus on the cost of investment products for a moment. Understanding how the cost of the product you purchase is paid for is important. In the case of mutual funds and some other products, you may never pay a fee but the payment is reflected in the return you receive, as described above. What you need to know is what the fee is, compared to your return. There are various ways of calculating this but in its simplest terms, are you getting value for your money? That can be quite subjective when you factor in the professional financial planning advice you may be receiving along with the investment advice. Nevertheless, I have found that many investors understand the value of the advice and service they are receiving. A few need to be reminded of the intangibles that cannot be factored into the price of a product. So it is the hard cost of the product and the additional but free cost of the service that must be considered. Both should have value that matches or exceeds the fees paid.

When you know the cost of the product together with the value of the service from your professional advisor, you can decide if you are getting a fair deal in return for the fees you pay. Ask your advisor to provide you a list of the services provided—it's often extensive, yet seamless. You should know what you are—or are not—tapping into. A series of questions you should ask appears at the end of this chapter.

SHOP AROUND: GET MORE INFORMATION

There are many sources of investor education that can help you with decision making and get better results for the professional dollars you pay. The *Master Your Personal Finance* books published by The Knowledge Bureau, of which this book is one in a series, is a good place to start. Consult the front and back pages of this book and visit www.knowledge-bureau.com for more information about new books in the series and self study courses you may take advantage of. Also, be sure to subscribe to *Breaking Tax* and *Investment News* which is a free weekly electronic publication published by The Knowledge Bureau that will give you the latest information on tax and economic trends to help you master your real wealth.

Specifically relating to the issue of fees, the World Wide Web can be a wealth of information, too. Simply googling 'investment fees in Canada' brings up millions of results. Be sure to look at the most recent information since the area of fees is constantly changing. Some websites that can help you with your research are:

- Investor Learning Centre—an independent, not-for-profit organization which provides non-promotional investment information to the general public. (https://www.credentialdirect.com/Education/ilc/InvestorLearning Centre.aspx)
- Morningstar Canada—an independent investment research firm. http://www.morningstar.ca/globalhome/marketinfo/ MarketInfo.asp?tab=invest
- Fund Library.com—An information resource sponsored by Canada's mutual fund companies. (http://www.fundlibrary.com/)
- Globefund—a source of unbiased mutual fund information. (http://www.globefund.com/)

Many of your financial institutions will also have information on this subject. The key is to take investment cost into account on both sides of the balance sheet: net growth of your assets over time is the number you are evaluating.

IN SUMMARY

THINGS YOU NEED TO KNOW

- The cost of investing can impact your real returns over time.
- Sometimes the cost of investing can be deducted on your income tax return.
- Carrying charges like investment management fees, interest costs, safety deposit box fees, and often a portion of your accounting and tax preparation fees can be tax deductible.
- Different fees are paid for different investment product types. These fees can be taken off before you receive your investment return, they can be deferred, they can be paid through hourly management fees or even a percentage of your capital. There can also be a commission for each trade you make. Find out the cost of buying and selling various assets before you invest.
- Often the fees for services you receive from your professional financial advisor are taken out of the imbedded cost of the investment; that is, you don't pay extra for the hours of service the professional provides to you. Be sure to understand the costs and value of services provided.
- When you "do it yourself" consider your trading costs over time, and put a value on your own time, knowledge, education and experience as well. It's when times are volatile or unpredictable that discipline, training, team discussion and knowledge pays off. Are you getting that when you work alone? Is there a price to be paid when you don't have access to information and experience?

QUESTIONS YOU NEED TO ASK

- Will I actually save money over time—and get better returns—if I manage my own money?
- What am I willing to pay for my investment activities?
- What services will I receive for fees I pay?
- What is the difference between commissioned services, fee-based services and fee-for-service advice?
- What is discretionary versus non-discretionary management?
- Will my fees include a strategic focus through a financial plan? Will I understand where my real wealth is today and what pathway I should take to accumulation and growth of assets in the future?
- Will I receive consistent follow up meetings to discuss the effect of investment activities on my personal net worth?
- Will my fees for services include a process for goal-setting and action plans for the future?
- Can I discuss in advance changes in my personal circumstances—loss of job or marriage for example? Are there extra fees for this?
- What are new product and tax efficiency solutions to help me manage lifecycle changes?
- How do I properly start and end a relationship with an advisor?
- What effect does moving my portfolio or switching my assets have on my costs?

THINGS YOU NEED TO DO

- Be prepared. Research fees for investment products and services before you decide on professional or do-it-yourself wealth management.
- Seek information about the cost of your investment activities on an annual basis to receive information for tax filing purposes.
- Interview different types of professional financial advisors and find out how they are compensated for the services they provide you.
- Tap into inter-professional advice and referrals—what does your accountant think of your potential financial advisor or lawyer, for example.

DECISIONS YOU NEED TO MAKE

- Should I manage my money myself or pay for professional money management?
- Do I need more investment advice to get the results I want?

MASTER YOUR REAL WEALTH
The Impact of Investment Cost

TIPS

- Understand how financial products are priced when purchasing them.
- Decide how actively you want to be involved in the portfolio management process.
- Pick the appropriate product based on your investment knowledge and risk profile while understanding the cost of the product.

TRAPS

- Never discount the value of advice.
- Recognize that active trading can have a cost, both in terms of fees but also by reduced returns.
- Don't try to do this "on the cheap". You get what you pay for.

Principle Mastery: To master your real wealth, you cannot leave out the cost of managing your investments in determining your long term wealth management plans. However, also remember that when you pay for professional services, you should receive the benefits of getting better integrated results. Discuss both fees and services—and the time value of money—in determining cost.

CHAPTER 11

How to Achieve Peace of Mind and Consistent Results

If you do not get it from yourself, where will you go for it? ZEN PROVERB

You've finally done it—you've set up an investment program and feel great about having taken that initiative. Yet your capital is being eroded—by taxes, inflation, currency and market volatility. Despite your best efforts, even your net worth statement seems to be suffering from these realities in the marketplace.

"How can I build and maximize and preserve my wealth to meet upcoming life events and my personal priorities, despite these numerous obstacles?"

That certainly seems to be the question of the day, no matter your age, investment knowledge or net worth. The truth is, things change, often rapidly. As I am writing this we are experiencing some of the worst financial markets in the past 30 years. Every-one's reaction to this varies, depending on their backgrounds, personal psyches, stage of life and their expectations.

Whether or not we can achieve some peace of mind is largely dependent on our understanding of how things will work out going forward. That requires a strategy, process and plan, working with top people who understand their client's vision, value and goals.

THE ISSUES

Specifically, this book has been written for:

- People who want to know how to foster the continued growth, preservation and transition of their accumulated capital by understanding principles of Real Wealth Management™
- People who want to work smarter with professional financial advisors to preserve and transition wealth to the next generation
- People who simply want to understand a bit more of the financial world

We hope you have a better understanding of some the most important wealth building principles and that you are now able to take whatever next steps you consider most appropriate for you.

Here is what I hope you have learned:

- **What is the importance of creating sustainable 'real' wealth?** 'Real' wealth—after taxes, inflation, costs and currency risk—is critical to managing your life events and preparing you for financial self-reliance in the future.
- **What are the principles of Real Wealth Management™?** Understanding how taxes, inflation, currency risk, investment fees and the intergenerational transfer of wealth impact on your net worth are key to building and preserving it.
- **Recognizing that your future goals are not individualistic.** They are interdependent and tied to the goals of those individuals important in your life.
- **Understanding how your emotions can intervene.** There are strategies to help but often the most valuable resource is your professional advisory team. If you are working on your own, don't let all the "noise" confuse you. Speak with friends and family to find out their opinions about events as well. And be sure to link your investment activities to a sound tax and estate plan.

- **The importance of establishing a base point from which you can determine the growth of your personal net worth.** Developing your own Personal Net Worth Statement and reviewing your cash flow to determine how you can re-allocate your resources more effectively is a critical element of analyzing and planning to build your 'real' wealth. It's a good snapshot of where you are today and a starting point for action planning to take new information and events into account.

- **Understanding the concepts of financial 'risk zones' and risk management.** Preserving wealth is as important as growing it. So is transitioning it. It's what you keep that counts.

- **How to work more effectively with key advisors and specialists on your financial team.** Asking questions and trying to understand the issues are important. It's okay to want to know and there is no such thing as a stupid question.

ASSESSING NEXT STEPS

Now that you have a better understanding of some of the most important wealth building principles and processes, you should be better equipped to make financial decisions on an ongoing basis, as markets ebb and flow and your lifecycle needs change. The key steps in initiating such decision making include the following:

1. Identify the issue of concern.
2. Complete some basic research on the subject so you have a better understanding of it.
3. Look to your Personal Net Worth Statement for any solutions it might offer you.
4. If you don't have a solution, or a plan, speak with an expert.
5. Implement the changes needed to address the issue.

In deciding what will work best for you in building 'real' wealth, using a consistent process in conjunction with an expert team of advisors can help.

The following are some of the key issues you will want to address as you move forward:

Work Alone or With an Expert Advisor

The first decision is to decide whether you want to go it alone or work with a professional advisor. Many professionals work very hard to stay on top of their field—the stream of new information is unrelenting. It may be very difficult for someone not working in the field full-time to stay current.

Understand Your Investor Personality

You may acknowledge that your investment personality is very emotional and that you tend to react to market changes with great angst. This is another good reason to work with someone who can keep you disciplined, and help you stick to a long term strategic plan.

Try to be honest with how you feel when markets go down—sharply. Cheating on your risk tolerance in order to try for a better return never works. The most likely outcome is a knee-jerk reaction that is detrimental to achieving your long term goals.

Start With Your Personal Net Worth Statement

This is the starting point for working on your own or with a financial professional. You may be able to take some corrective steps by yourself: brown bag your lunches for a few days of the week/buy a slightly used car instead of a new one. Understanding the difference between depreciating assets and wealth building assets and discretionary and non-discretionary expenses are vital to growing your real wealth.

Understand the Data

Do you know what you need to know and what you should do? Some understanding of the financial arena is important or you may not be able to recognize if the information you are receiving makes any sense. An easy way to start is to look at headlines in the business pages or watch the news hour on TV. Challenge yourself to listen mindfully to topics as they relate to financial issues.

Determine What Changes Need to be Made

Perhaps your portfolio could benefit from asset or product allocation. Not sure what to do? Don't hesitate to work with an investment professional. The correct asset allocation is a significant factor on the investment return of your portfolio. If you are unsure how to minimize your income taxes, a tax professional can help you to identify changes that can be made.

Implement

This is the hardest part. You have the information—now you need to make some changes. Try remembering the goal(s) you are trying to achieve and what that will mean to you—this may not make it easier to change but it may help to keep you determined.

Remembering What is Important to You

You started out on this journey because there is something important to you. There is a goal you wish to achieve, a future you envision. At all times, remember this. It will make some of the discipline that is required easier to accept and it will keep you focused. There will be others affected by your decisions and for whom you will be making decisions. Getting their input and agreement will make your plan that much stronger.

It's Never Too Late to Ask for Help

It has been my experience that no matter when you ask for help, it's never too late. You might not have as much time to make adjustments but at least you will know your options and can make some informed decisions.

There is an old proverb that says happiness will result when expectations equal reality. If you ask for help to get to your reality, there is a greater certainty that your expectations will be met. The best relationships between professionals and their clients are partnerships, with responsibilities on both sides. Discuss your expectations with your advisor and ask about your advisor's expectations. With this understood, you have laid a solid foundation for moving forward.

Timely Reviews

This is a by-product of establishing your expectations. Not everyone wants to meet with their advisor on a regular basis; some only want email updates while others favour face to face meetings. This is the most important part of the professional relationship since it helps determine the communication lines that each party prefers.

A little advance preparation can help you make the most of these meetings. Let your advisor know what you would like to discuss and ask if there are any issues he or she feels are important for you to review at this time. Your advisor will already have items planned which he or she would like to review at the time of your meeting but it's very useful for him or her to know if there are any issues or concerns you have that can be prepared for and addressed when you get together. Sometimes this will be a review of plans already in place and other times there may be new issues that have just come up. The more your financial professional knows about you, the more he or she can help you prepare for.

Enjoy Each Chapter of Your Life. Life presents us with many challenges and joys. I honestly believe that you cannot give up everything today for the possibility of what may happen tomorrow. What if tomorrow does not come? But the tradeoff must be done responsibly. If you enjoy travelling, waiting until you retire to do so may a mistake. In a study by Desjardins Financial Security entitled *"Perfect Garden, The Psychology of Retirement"*, exotic travel during retirement was the most popular dream for 48% of Canadian full-time and part-time workers over 40 years old. The number one dream Canadians have when they retire is to remain healthy. Travel takes a back seat post-retirement, at 24%.

Living in the moment can be difficult to do; yet it is remarkably easier if you have a plan in place. You know your goals, you have taken action and you understand where you are right now. You may not be able to coast into the future but you are much better equipped to deal with life events that affect us all.

I sincerely hope you have learned a method to break free of stress relating to the future of your money so you can focus on living your dreams. I wish you well as you move through and into each life chapter. It can be exciting and very fulfilling when you reach your goals.

MASTER YOUR REAL WEALTH
How to Achieve Peace of Mind and Consistent Results

TIPS

- Decide if you can go it alone or would benefit from working with a financial professional.
- Review the principles of Real Wealth Management™ to ascertain how your personal net worth is being impacted.
- Recognize your investment personality and how you can manage it so as to not sabotage your long-term goals.
- Continue to familiarize yourself with important financial planning concepts.

TRAPS

- Don't be afraid to ask for help and never think it is too late to do so.
- Don't establish your goals in isolation—consult the important people in your life.
- Don't become overwhelmed by changes—chop things down into manageable portions and remember what is important to you.
- Don't forget to implement! Get help if you need to.

Principle Mastery: Master your real wealth—after tax, inflation and cost— but take the time to enjoy it too.

Index

Other Titles in
The Knowledge Bureau's
Master Your Series

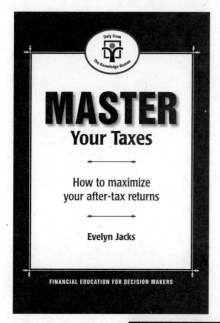